BIRD
BEE
&BUG
HOUSES

BIRD BEE & BUG HOUSES

DEREK JONES

simple projects for your garden

GUILD OF MASTER
CRAFTSMAN PUBLICATIONS

First published 2010 by
Guild of Master Craftsman Publications Ltd
Castle Place, 166 High Street, Lewes,
East Sussex BN7 1XU

ISBN: 978-1-86108-644-0

Associate Publisher Jonathan Bailey
Production Manager Jim Bulley
Managing Editor Gerrie Purcell
Senior Project Editor Virginia Brehaut
Copy Editor Nicola Hodgson
Technical Writer Rob Yarham
Managing Art Editor Gilda Pacitti
Design Chloë Alexander

Step-by-step photographs by Derek Jones
Cut out photographs by Anthony Bailey
Exploded diagrams by Simon Rodway
Styled photography by Rebecca Mothersole

Additional pictures from:

Flickr.com: p5 peasap, p10 Velo Steve, p32 (top) imcountingfoz,
p36 kevincole, p40 law keven, p46 OliBac, p52 Thundercheese,
p58 Oakley Originals, p64 kevincole, p70 ibm4381, p84 and p90
U.S. Fish and Wildlife Service, p98 BobMacinnes, p104 jbaker5,
p110 MarilynJane, p118 David Prior, p124 jbaker5, p130 mikebaird,
p136 kerryhjames, p142 peasap, p148 photogirl7

iStockphoto.com: p2 Galina Ermolaeva, p9 Andrew Howe,
p78 Tadeusz Przybyl, p160 Michael Stubblefield

Morguefile.com: p30 mrmac04

Set in Nofret and Helvetica Neue
Colour origination by GMC Reprographics
Printed and bound by Polygraf in Slovakia

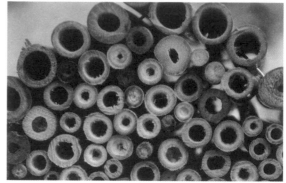

Contents

Getting started

Bee houses

Birdhouses

Bat houses

Bug houses

Introduction

I should come clean straight away and say that when I was asked to write this book, my enthusiasm for backyard wildlife was by no means matched by my knowledge of the subject. Sensing there was more I could do to encourage wildlife in my garden than simply scattering crusts on the lawn and topping up the birdbath soon had me rummaging around in the shed. As I have been known to make the odd piece of furniture, I figured that I was at least half-way qualified for the challenge of producing boxes and houses to encourage wildlife to take up residence in my garden. The process of creating the projects for this book has certainly given me increased awareness of and appreciation for the things that go on in and around my garden as a result. I hope that sharing this information will have tremendous benefits as well.

The projects in this book are suitable for a broad range of skills. They range from making simple log-pile structures for bees to constructing des-res terraced housing for sparrows. Each project has step-by-step instructions and offers ideas for variations to create functional and stylish accommodation for a wide range of garden wildlife. In addition to houses for birds, bees and bugs, this book also has a bonus section on bat houses.

I have prepared a list of the tools that you will need, as well as suitable materials and all the necessary techniques to get you started and perhaps pave the way for some of the more demanding projects.

Many of the materials featured you may already have piled up in the shed or left over from basic home-improvement projects around the house. Some materials you may need to buy, and I have made sure that these are easily obtainable from a number of sources.

It would be unfair to take full credit for these projects; many of them would have been impossible without the help of Mark Baker and Anthony Bailey. Their contribution has been greater than either of them would like to admit.

Getting started

Tools

All but one of the projects in this book can be made using just the basic hand–tools that are commonplace in most well–stocked DIY stores. There are as many ways to work wood as there are tools to work with and you will by no means need every tool listed here; one or two from each of the following categories should be enough.

▲ As well as squares, a straight edge rule and a marking gauge may well come in handy.

Marking out straight lines
Squares are available in a variety of sizes. They are used to create straight lines or to check that lines and edges are perpendicular to one another.

Marking angles and curves
Some squares are set at angles other than 90 degrees. The most common, known as a mitre square, is set at 45 degrees. A sliding bevel is an adjustable device that allows you to capture or set any angle. A protractor will do much the same thing. A pair of dividers will mark out curves.

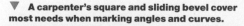

▼ A carpenter's square and sliding bevel cover most needs when marking angles and curves.

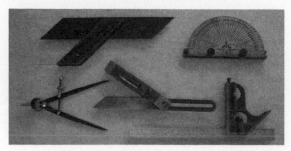

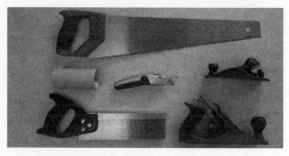

▲ Cutting and shaping tools can be bought from all well-stocked DIY stores.

Cutting and shaping
A panel saw is useful for cutting sheet material as well as solid timber. Smaller pieces of wood and bamboo are easier to cut using a smaller saw with finer teeth. Bench planes can be used to shape and flatten edges. Medium to coarse abrasive paper will be handy to remove jagged edges.

Assembly
Bar clamps, F–clamps and spring clamps are extremely useful around the workshop. Use them to hold things in place while gluing and to secure

▼ Clamps are as essential to your tool kit as are hammers and screwdrivers.

▲ Cordless jigsaw (left) and a circular saw (right).

▲ Ear defenders, dust masks and safety goggles should all be used when appropriate.

work while it is being cut or drilled. Having the right tool for the job extends to hammers and screwdrivers as well.

Cutting

Jigsaws and circular saws, whether corded or cordless, can be used to cut timber and sheet material. Some jobs can be done with either tool, but other tasks are specific to each machine. A jigsaw can cut along a curved line as well as a straight one. A circular saw can cut to a pre-set depth and straight lines, but not curves.

Drilling

Drills come in all shapes and sizes, both corded and cordless. The largest of the new generation of cordless drills are powerful enough to cope with drilling large entrance holes, and have batteries

▼ An 18v combination drill/driver and a smaller 10.8v version.

that can often be completely recharged in under 30 minutes. A good selection of driver bits makes the investment in one of these more worthwhile.

Safety equipment

Don't forget that working with wood can be potentially hazardous. Basic PPE (Personal Protection Equipment) is a must and will help minimize some of the risks.

Specialist tools

For the more adventurous, a router is a versatile machine that can simplify some tasks and speed things up. Nail guns can also make some tasks easier. They work by using compressed air either from a replaceable gas canister contained in the tool or from a reservoir linked to a compressor.

▼ A plunge router with a ¼in (6mm) collet will cope with all the projects in this book.

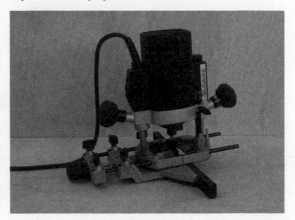

Materials

All of the projects in this book are fairly small-scale, and are ideally suited for using up leftover and scrap materials from larger projects. The houses and boxes can all be made from easily sourced materials; apart from timber and roofing materials, all you will need are adhesives and fixings.

Timber and sheet material

The most widely available sheet material suitable for making nesting boxes and bug houses is exterior or marine-grade plywood. Perhaps easier to come by is rough-sawn and prepared solid timber. Timber yards and builders' merchants stock a variety of moulded timber that is easily incorporated into small-scale projects. DIY stores are also an excellent resource for small-section timber products.

Leftover material

At the end of every maintenance job there is leftover material perfect for constructing nesting boxes. Self-adhesive flooring tiles can be used on the roof of a birdhouse to simulate stone or slate. Mineralized roofing felt and lead also have their uses, as does faux grass. Bamboo canes and other dried-out plant stems, with their hollow interiors, are ideal spaces for bugs and bees.

▼ Prepared timber products can often be obtained with a ready-made profile to simplify construction.

Recycled materials

A stack of unwanted pallets like these contain perfect lengths of wood for many of the smaller projects in this book.

▲ Check all recycled materials to make sure any nails, screws or staples have been removed.

Wood thickness

The British Trust for Ornithology (BTO) advises that any wood used to make birdhouses is at least ⅝in (15mm) thick in order to provide sufficient insulation.

▲ Logs are a very useful material for making bug or bee houses. You may even come across some of the species you are trying to attract in an existing pile of logs.

Lost and found

Logs, twigs and branches can make an ideal starting point for building a bug or bee house.

Adhesives

Any adhesives that you use should be exterior grade and used sparingly. PVAs and polyurethane variants are readily available. Clean any traces off the internal faces of bird and bat boxes. Make sure adhesives have properly cured/dried before putting the box to use. Spray adhesives are unsuitable for joining wood but are good for attaching some roofing products. A hot–melt glue will also do the job.

Fixings

Any screws, nails, hinges and hooks that you use should be rust–resistant. Stainless steel, brass or galvanized steel are perfect for outdoor use.

▼ All of these fixings are available in small packs in most well-stocked DIY stores.

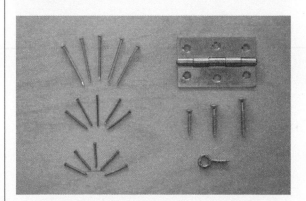

Unsuitable materials

Avoid materials that have been processed with timber-preserving chemicals. These can generally be easily identified by the khaki green colour towards the outer edges. MDF and chipboard are also unsuitable.

Cutting angles, curves and grooves

The projects in this book are quite straightforward, but you will need to know how to prepare the shaped pieces for the houses and boxes by cutting your timber into angled and curved forms. Some of the projects also require you to cut grooves into the wood.

Angles

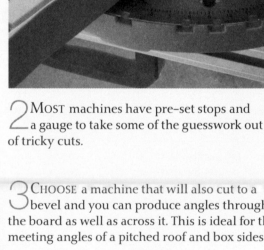

1 THE best way to accurately cut repeat angles is with a machine. A cross–cut saw (sometimes called a compound mitre saw) will make things much easier.

2 MOST machines have pre–set stops and a gauge to take some of the guesswork out of tricky cuts.

3 CHOOSE a machine that will also cut to a bevel and you can produce angles through the board as well as across it. This is ideal for the meeting angles of a pitched roof and box sides.

4 A table saw is a larger machine that can be used to reduce whole sheets of board.

5 CHOOSE one with a tilting arbour, and with the correct cross-cutting attachment you will be able to cut angles as well.

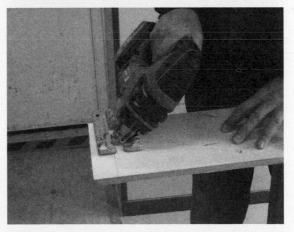

6 FOR something more manageable, you could use a portable circular saw. Most have the ability to cut angles as well as straight cuts. Use a straight edge at first until you gain confidence and are able to follow a pencil line freehand.

7 MOST jigsaws also allow you to cut angles by adjusting the base-plate.

Curves

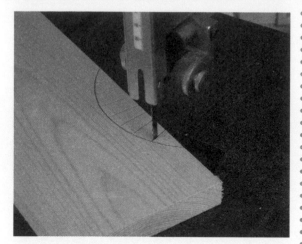

1 CURVES are best cut using a machine, either a jigsaw or band–saw. Whichever you use – and the finer the blade the better – make some cuts in from the edge of the material to the line of the curve. This technique works for cutting either side of the line.

2 ON the band–saw, begin to cut along the line. The waste material will fall away in segments, reducing the likelihood of damaging the blade, and will result in a much cleaner cut. If you find you are running off–line and need to back up a little you will not have so far to get to an 'escape line'. On smaller machines this reversing can sometimes derail the blade.

3 PINCHING the blade on either machine will cause overheating, which will shorten the life of the blade and in extreme cases scorch the material. Jigsaws are more likely to wander off–line when forced, preferring to follow the grain rather than the line. On thicker material, make half of the cut across the grain first.

4 THEN complete the line from the other end. Tight curves will need the exit lines closer together. Always wait until the blade has stopped moving before lifting the jigsaw off the job.

Grooves

1 A jig will make cutting grooves much easier, whether you do them by hand or with a machine. Make a simple T-square by screwing a piece of thin plywood or MDF to another, thicker piece of timber with one edge at 90 degrees.

2 WITH the right cutter in the router, run the machine against the fence of the T-square along the straight edge of the base-plate, making a cut that mimics the groove into the cross of the T-square.

3 MARK lines on the finished component for the grooves and use the one you have created on the jig to line up for the real ones on the job.

4 IF you don't have a router, use the same jig to make the cuts with a handsaw.

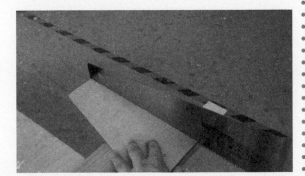

5 THIS time, run the saw against the edge of the T. It will keep your fingers well out of the way of the blade and result in nice straight lines.

6 THE same jig can be used with a circular saw set to the appropriate depth to run along the edge of the base-plate, as with the router.

Jointing and assembly

The jointing and construction methods for the projects are very basic; there aren't any joints in the strict sense. This can make things tricky to line up, as there is little in the way of mechanical assistance to hold things in place while gluing, screwing or nailing.

Marking lines

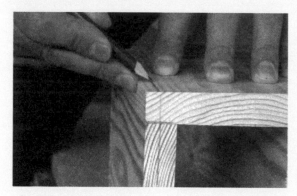

1 MARKING out where to put holes for screws and where to drive in nails helps prevent them splitting the timber and bursting through the sides of the box. Use a finger as a depth gauge against a pencil to transfer lines from the centre of one piece to another.

2 A marking gauge will do the same job. It can be set to give a reference point for the duration of the project. It will also come in handy for marking lines that are out of reach of fingers.

Drills and pilot holes for screws

1 DRILLING holes for screws prevents timber from splitting, but the holes need to be the right size for the joint to close tight. The first hole is through the piece of timber that is being fixed. It needs to be roughly the same size as the screw, including its thread. Too small and the thread will bite and prevent the joint from closing; too big and the head of the screw will pull through the timber as it is tightened.

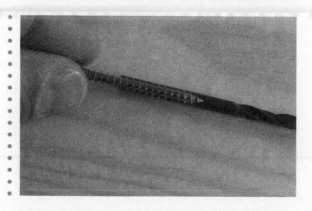

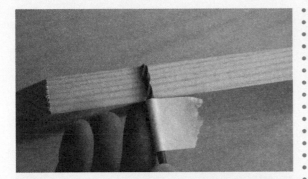

2 YOU may decide to drill this hole while you are holding the two pieces together. Wrap some tape around the drill bit as a marker to avoid drilling into the other piece of timber.

3 A few extra winds of tape and this marker will act as a temporary depth stop for a few holes before wearing away.

4 PUT the screws into the first holes and position the piece of timber in place on the other piece. Give them a tap with a hammer so that they leave a mark on the corresponding piece, indicating where to drill the second hole.

5 THE second hole needs to be the same size as the core of the screw without the thread. It is drilled into the piece of timber to which the first piece is being attached.

Nailing

1 GALVANIZED or zinc-coated nails are for external use (left). Panel pins (centre) have a head that is too small and will rust and come loose quite quickly. Oval nails (right) are widely used in carpentry because the shape is less likely to split the wood. The small heads are also much easier to drive below the surface for filling in before any final finishing is done.

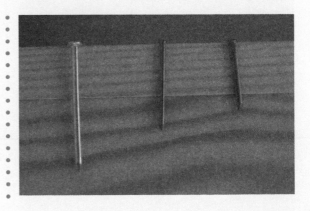

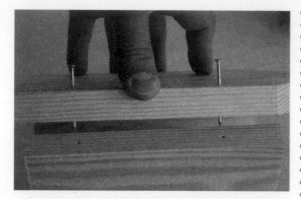

2 ALTHOUGH nails are quick and convenient to use, they do not make for a lasting weather–tight joint. For this you will also need to use glue. To prevent things from sliding around while you hit the nails home, drive them in a little way first so that a small hole is created in the corresponding piece of wood. Use the holes to relocate the two pieces after applying some glue.

3 A nail gun is a fabulous tool for achieving results quickly. Some components can be tricky to align without having fingers close to where the pins will be fired. Use tape to hold things in place so the work can be done safely.

Gluing up

THERE are two main types of glue that are suitable and readily available. The first is polyurethane (sometimes called PU) glue (below, top). It is treacly in appearance and cures when exposed to moisture. It foams and expands during this process and can even force the two

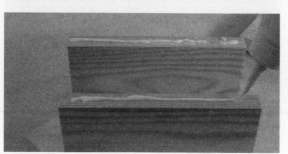

mating surfaces apart if they are not fixed in some way. It also leaves unpleasant black stains on the skin that are difficult to remove, so wear protective gloves while working with it. Different brands have different drying times.

The second widely available glue is PVA (left, bottom). Although white in colour, it dries clear and can be washed off the skin quite easily. Again, different brands have different drying times.

Hot–melt glue (below) is an excellent adhesive for attaching flexible materials in place. It is weatherproof and cures quickly as it cools. For this reason, it is not suitable for joining the main components together as there is little time for lining things up or putting in screws.

Edge jointing

To make the most of off-cuts and recycled timber, it may be necessary to join two or more pieces together along the edge. This step-by-step guide will help you achieve this without gaps and without the use of clamps.

1 THE piece of timber on the right has a square edge that is rough and has a slight bow in the middle. The piece on the left has a smooth straight edge but is not square.

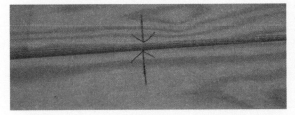

2 LAY the two pieces face down and make a mark across the intended joint line.

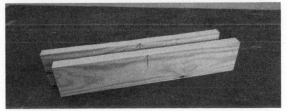

3 STAND the two pieces up with the pencil marks on the same side and pointing in the same direction.

4 PUT the pieces together in a vice and plane the two edges as if one. Try to get a straight edge along the length of the timber.

5 IT is not critical to achieve a perfectly square edge across the two pieces so long as it is even along the length.

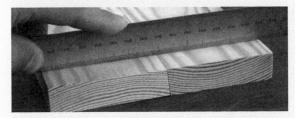

6 LAY the two pieces face down on the bench with the planed edges together. Turn one of them over. You will now have two edges that can be glued together to make a single flat board.

7 APPLY glue to one edge and press the two pieces together, rubbing up and down until you detect some resistance to the movement. Align the two pieces and secure with tape.

Drilling holes

Drilling small holes in timber for screws is quite straightforward, but drilling larger ones to form the entrance holes to the houses can be a little tricky. You need the right drill bit or tool for the job, for which there are a few options available. All will work with a reasonably sized and well–charged cordless drill as well as a corded one. Some work only in a fixed drill, while others must not be used in this way.

Drills and drill bits

1 THE drills shown here are best described using their generic names rather than any trade names, which may be confusing or misleading. Anti–clockwise from the top: hole–saw, flat bit, auger, borer and regular wood drill bits.

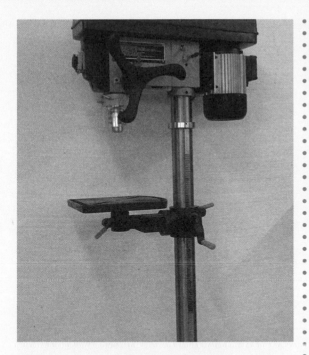

2 PILLAR drills like this one will give you the best results. They are versatile machines that do not take up too much room in a workshop. A bench-top version will be cheaper than a floor-standing one.

4 THE side grip on most hand drills is attached around a 43mm–diameter collar. When removed, the drill can be mounted onto the apparatus to achieve an effective drill press.

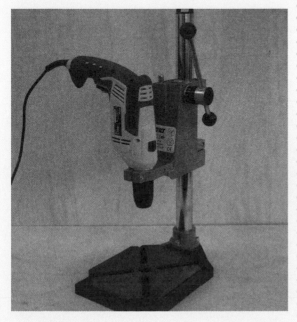

5 FOR stability, fix the press to the bench with screws or bolts or even clamps. To increase the size of the drill bed and to make life simpler, prepare some off–cuts of timber to the height of the existing bed.

3 THIS set–up is even cheaper. It makes use of a hand drill mounted onto a bench top press.

6 THESE needn't be fixed, but will act as packing to support a longer piece of timber on which to rest the pieces being drilled.

Hole-saws

1 HOLE-SAWS can be used in a handheld drill because they have a centring bit to prevent skating around the surface before the hole is established. Different sizes of hole-saw are attached to a separate arbour. Use a suitable piece of off-cut material to avoid any contact between the drill base and the hole-saw.

2 IN some engineered materials, hole-saws can smoke a bit if run at too fast a speed. Because of the amount of surface area in contact with the material being cut, these saws have a tendency to snatch and catch the user by surprise if you begin to lean in any direction part-way through. Clamp the job in place to avoid this if using a pillar drill. Handheld machines should be fitted with a side grip.

Flat bits

1 FLAT bits can be used in a handheld drill as they have a centring point. For a clean hole on exit, support the job behind with a piece of scrap thick enough to absorb the centring point.

2 FLAT bits need to run at a fast speed to achieve a clean hole and are easy to line up with any pencil line that marks the spot.

Augers

1 AUGERS come with one, two or three spirals around a threaded centring pin that grabs the material and pulls the bit through to the other side. Very little lateral force is required to drill the hole, as the bit is designed to do most of the work. Augers can only be used in a handheld drill at slow speed and are not to be used in a fixed drill.

2 CLAMPING the job to the bench with a scrap piece beneath is essential, as you will need both hands to hold the drill safely.

3 THE finished result is fairly crude and will need a little smoothing with a suitable abrasive paper.

Entrance holes

You can attract a range of bird species to your birdhouse by drilling different-sized entrance holes. For a general guide to which birds prefer which hole sizes, see pages 36–37.

Borers

1 THIS type of bit is called a borer. It cannot be used in a handheld drill and needs to be run at a fast speed while making slow progress through the material to achieve a clean hole.

2 A borer is not the easiest bit to align with any marks that you may have made, but does give a very clean hole.

3 CLAMPING the job in place is a must when using a borer. A block of wood clamped or screwed in position to act as a location for multiple holes will speed up the process and make the procedure much safer.

4 THIS type of borer is also only suitable for use in a fixed drill. The rather coarse teeth cut quickly but leave a rough finish.

Smaller bits

1 LIP and spur bits like this are good for drilling smaller holes. The spur helps to align the drill with any marks you may have made.

2 STANDARD drill bits are more than adequate for most small holes that do not require a great level of accuracy.

Finishing

It is not necessary to apply a finish to your bird, bee or bug house for it to appeal to its intended occupants, but it can help to prolong the life of the house. Non-toxic, water-based stains are preferable as potential finishes for your bird, bee or bug house but some oil-based products can also be used. Any type of finish should be applied only to the exterior. Some oil-based preservatives, such as creosote, contain chemicals that are harmful to wildlife, so take care when selecting any type of finishing product.

WHEN painting a bird box, make sure that you cover the entrance hole before applying a paint finish so as to prevent any over-spray getting on the hole or inside the box. Chemicals in some preservatives may be harmful to wildlife after long-term exposure. It is also generally accepted that bats are less tolerant of finishes than birds are.

Water-based stains or dyes are available in standard wood colours as well as more exciting, less natural tones such as red and even vibrant greens and blues. As well as conventional paints, some oil-based textured finishes are available as aerosols. The natural tones and textures mimic stone and metal quite convincingly. Oil-based preservatives are available in many different shades but tend to come in fairly large quantities. Applied with a brush, oil-based paints can appear a bit thick and gloopy, so try rubbing a small amount in with a cloth and allowing each coat to dry before applying a second or third coat to achieve the desired colour. Small sample pots are a good idea, but they can be an expensive way of buying a product. Be sure to take care when using leftover tins of product since they may have important information obscured by spills on the labelling.

Whatever preservatives or finishes you use, make sure that the boxes have dried completely before putting them up so that there is no wet residue or potentially harmful fumes.

▼ **Water-based stains will allow the character of the wood to show through.**

Choosing colours

Consider the location of your box when choosing a colour for your finish. A dark colour will absorb and retain heat far more than a lighter colour. In some instances this may be desirable, but never place a dark-coloured box in a site that will be exposed to sunlight at the warmest time of day.

Where to hang the houses

Before you embark on any of the projects in this book, think carefully about possible sites for the houses. Different species have different needs for the site of their nesting box or shelter. Ignore these needs and your house may never become occupied.

Birdhouses

BIRDHOUSES, however well planned, are not the natural habitat for birds, so it pays to choose your site wisely if all your efforts are not to be wasted. The box should be sited where the comings and goings of the birds cannot be observed by predators. If you want to see birds in action, consider providing a feeding station near by so you can watch and enjoy a whole range of birds.

The chosen location should be inaccessible to predators such as domestic cats, larger predatory birds and even squirrels. If you put the box in a tree, be sure not to place it where there is a convenient branch or ledge for intruders to perch close to the entrance hole. Birdhouses should always be placed at least 6ft (2m) above the ground. Choose a site away from areas of traffic as well as people.

Where possible, the site should be out of direct sunlight or at least facing north. Birds are better suited to coping with cold conditions than sweltering heat. The entrance should face away from the prevailing wind.

Remember that your birdhouse will need to be cleaned out at least once a year. Choose a site that will not be difficult to access. The ideal time for hanging your box is immediately after the breeding season in the autumn, but a well–sited box may attract interest in early spring.

▶ **A good site for a bird box, out of the reach of any predators that may be lurking.**

Empty houses

You may find that your house is ignored for the first year, or sometimes longer. Do not be discouraged – some species need plenty of time to get used to the house before the breeding season begins.

Bat houses

THE most successful location for a bat box is on a tree. Try siting three boxes facing in different directions, with a clear path to each box. Bats like to move from one box to another during the day and from season to season as temperatures change. Choose a position as high as you can safely reach, ideally above 16ft (5m).

The main concerns for building a successful bat box are good insulation and the avoidance of damp and draughts. Bats are more sensitive to these requirements than to the material used for the construction. Heat and humidity should remain a constant level – that means tight joints and a thick solid material for the top.

For the best chance of attracting bats to your box, choose a site where bats are known to feed, such as woodland and river banks. Some parkland can also be suitable; select a sheltered spot out of the blast of strong winds but exposed to sunlight for as much of the day as possible.

Bats use the natural landscape to navigate and some are reluctant to cross open spaces to go between roosts. For this reason, choose a site in close proximity to a tree or hedge line.

Although a solitary box can attract bats, a group or cluster of boxes in a suitable location is likely to have greater appeal. Boxes can be sited on buildings, which can provide protection from bad weather. Somewhere quiet is the rule here. It is not uncommon for bats to take a while to investigate new premises, although if your box has not been occupied within three years you should consider moving it. Under no circumstances be tempted to open up a box if you suspect it is being occupied. Instead, look for other signs of habitation such as staining at the base of the box or crumbly brown or black droppings on the ground below.

Do not disturb

In the UK, it is illegal to disturb roosting bats at any time of year.

▼ **Bat houses should be hung at a height of at least 5m (16ft) from the ground.**

Bee houses

CHOOSE a site appropriate to the kind of bee you want to attract. This may be close to the ground or suspended from a tree. For solitary bees, the eaves of an outbuilding might make a good choice as it will be protected from the elements and less likely to be disturbed. There are no real height restrictions, so a balcony with plants or flowers would be equally suitable. Whatever the site, make sure that the bee house won't be disturbed for the period of hibernation.

Most bumblebees prefer to nest near the ground, so place your bumblebee box in position so that the entrance is close to the ground, but raise the box slightly so that it does not flood. The box should be positioned in a warm but sheltered position, such as along the edge of a fence or hedge, and not in direct sunlight. You can also cover the box with old vegetation.

▶ **Houses for solitary bees should be sited somewhere where they will be undisturbed.**

Bug houses

As with bees, there are no height restrictions on the location for bug houses intended for winged insects, providing there are sufficient food sources to attract them in the first place. A well-made insect box can sit comfortably on a balcony or be attached to a wall and not look out of place. They can be rather heavy, so be sure to fasten them down. Choose a warm spot that is unlikely to be disturbed, and make allowance for drainage. Ideally, site the box where it will be protected from the elements but not hidden. Ground-dwelling insects are unlikely to venture off the beaten track. If you prefer not to have your bugs on display, a small bunch of twigs tied together can be placed amid the foliage of an established planter. Secure them so they are not blown away or battered about in the wind.

▶ **Hanging height is less of an issue for bug houses but consider if you would like to attract mainly winged insects or ground-dwelling bugs as this may affect the position that you choose.**

How to hang the houses

It is probably easiest to attach a nesting box of any type to a man–made structure rather than to a tree or other natural location. A trip to your local hardware store should leave you with a few options, most of which will be in the form of a bracket. Look out for brass, galvanized or stainless steel fittings, as they won't rust.

Brackets and fixings

▲ This slotted bracket gives you a little leeway for adjustment up or down.

▲ This keyhole bracket is widely used as a fixing for pictures and mirrors, but is also suitable for use outside.

▲ This L-bracket can be used to support the weight of a heavier box. It will not be sufficient on its own – another bracket will be required at the top.

▲ For a small box, create a 'keyhole' with two different sized drills in the back panel. Fix the screw into the wall and fit the box over the screw. If the keyhole is in line with the entrance hole on the front you can tighten the screw through the hole with a long screwdriver.

▲ This galvanized steel post bracket is ideal for mounting a box on top of a post. Consider the location of the post first, as an exposed site will be vulnerable to extreme weather conditions.

▲ This lift-off-style bracket will allow the box to be removed from its location for cleaning and for any maintenance that may be necessary to the structure it is attached to. This is a good choice for larger boxes.

▲ These triangular corner brackets are designed for the construction of cabinetwork, but used in this fashion serve as a cradle for a larger box. An additional fixing at the top will be necessary.

▲ U-bolts like these can be used to attach a box to a pole or stake. The box needs to be fastened to a batten first, so strictly speaking it is the batten that is fixed to the pole.

Fixing onto trees

Attaching boxes to trees with screws or nails is an option, although it is not without its problems. Screws and nails can become loose as the tree grows and the branch expands, so a regular check needs to be part of your maintenance routine. A wooden dowel or peg makes a good alternative. Better still is a piece of chain attached to the box and slid inside a rubber hose, which will not cause damage to the tree. Avoid thin wires since these can become embedded in the tree as it grows and could present a serious hazard to a machinist in the future. Avoid using nails and screws for siting boxes in commercial woodland. Rogue nails and screws can cause damage to woodworking machines and be extremely dangerous for an unsuspecting machinist.

Battens

1 SPLIT battens are a popular choice for fixing cabinets or mirrors to a wall and would work just as well outdoors. Take a length of timber and cut down the middle along its length at 45 degrees. Fix one half of the batten to the back of the box, creating a hook out of the pointed edge pointing down.

2 FIX the other piece of the batten to the wall with the hook facing up. Now hang the box on the batten. This is a great way of trying out different types of boxes in the same location or even creating a terrace of boxes for house sparrows.

Birdhouse entrance hole sizes

This table is a general guide only to give you an idea of which common bird species prefer large or small entrance holes to their nesting sites. Natural nest holes are not always exactly the same size – it is more important that your birdhouse is secure, weatherproof and as safe as possible from predators than for the dimensions to be mathematically precise.

▼ Bluebirds prefer a small- to medium-sized entrance hole, which may also attract tree swallows or hairy woodpeckers.

Diameter of entrance hole	Common UK species	Common US species
1in (25mm)	blue tit, coal tit, marsh tit	
1⅛in (28mm)	great tit, tree sparrow, pied flycatcher	warbler, chickadee
1¼in (32mm)	house sparrow, nuthatch	nuthatch, titmouse, finches, downy woodpecker, house wren, Bewick's wren, Carolina wren
1½in (38mm)		bluebird, tree swallow, hairy woodpecker, yellow-bellied sapsucker, Carolina wren, ash-throated flycatcher
1¾in (45mm)	starling	flycatcher
2in (51mm)	great-spotted woodpecker	red-headed woodpecker
2¼in (57mm)		purple martin
2½in (64mm)	green woodpecker	northern flicker, Lewis's woodpecker
3in (76mm)		screech owl, American kestrel
6in (152mm)	stock dove, jackdaw	barn owl
Species that prefer an open-fronted house or shelf	robin, pied wagtail, spotted flycatcher, wren, blackbird, kestrel	barn swallow, American robin, phoebes

Bird-houses

Open-fronted birdhouse

This nest box was made from ¾in–thick (19mm) prepared timber bought from a builders' merchants. It has a roof made from broken slate roof tiles that would otherwise have been thrown away.

SOME birds prefer an open–fronted nesting box to the more usual type with a circular entrance hole. They are suitable for species such as robins, wrens and flycatchers or phoebes, barn swallows or American robins in the US – these last two American birds usually prefer larger openings or even a box with no front at all. You will need to choose the location for this box with care; this is the case for all birdhouses, but the inhabitants of open–fronted boxes are more exposed and therefore potentially more vulnerable to the weather and predators.

Species to expect

This nest box might become home to:

UK species – robin (right), wren, pied wagtail, spotted flycatcher.

US species – phoebe, barn swallow, American robin.

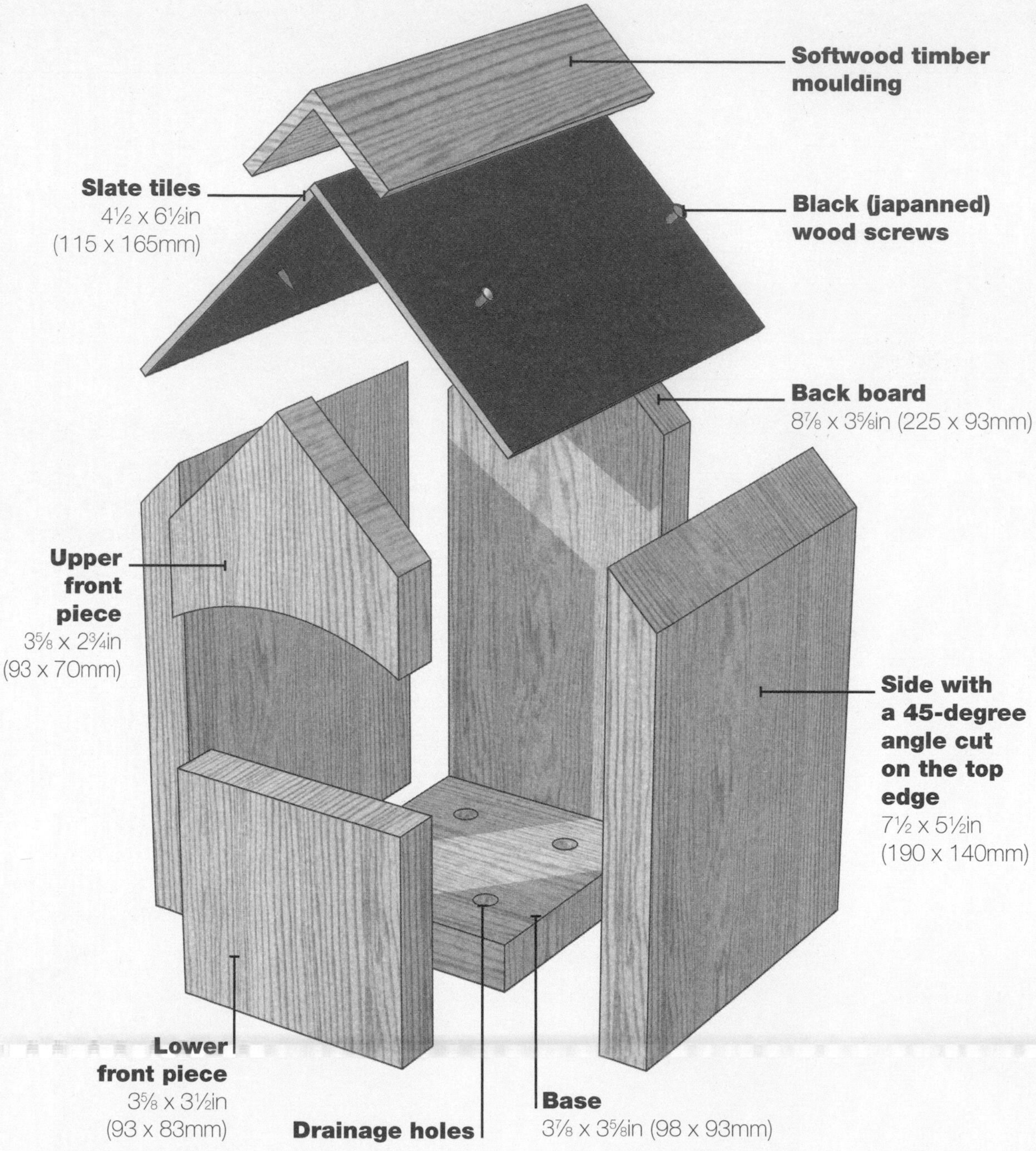

Softwood timber moulding

Slate tiles
4½ x 6½in
(115 x 165mm)

Black (japanned) wood screws

Back board
8⅞ x 3⅝in (225 x 93mm)

Upper front piece
3⅝ x 2¾in
(93 x 70mm)

Side with a 45-degree angle cut on the top edge
7½ x 5½in
(190 x 140mm)

Lower front piece
3⅝ x 3½in
(93 x 83mm)

Drainage holes

Base
3⅞ x 3⅝in (98 x 93mm)

Materials needed

¾in (19mm) prepared softwood timber
Slate roofing tiles
Corner edge moulding
Silicone adhesive

Cutting list

Front and back 8⅞ x 3⅝in (225 x 93mm)
Sides 7½ x 5½in (190 x 140mm)
Base 3⅞ x 3⅝in (98 x 93mm)
Roof 4½ x 6½in (115 x 165mm)

1 WHEN working with angles and shaped components that need to marry up neatly, it is a good idea to produce a template. This also means that duplicates can be made of the same item without you having to do the maths for a second time.

Box-building tip

This box is particularly suitable for fixing in position through the back via the large opening in the front. Just make sure all the components are flush at the back.

2 AN off cut of MDF or ply will work well for the template and create clear lines to cut to.

3 THERE are no awkward angles to cut on this nest box: a 90–degree and a 45–degree square are all that are required.

4 HAVING cut your components, assemble them for a dry fit. Drill holes for the screws, and with them in place, mark the pilot holes in the corresponding piece with a gentle tap from a hammer.

5 WHEN dismantling everything, you may need to undo the screws a little if they have bitten slightly. Drill the pilot holes and begin reassembling the components, starting with the back, base and front sections.

6 THE side components need an angle cut along the top edge. Mark the precise position for these off the back section. If you are cutting these by hand, transfer the marks around each face and edge using the two squares.

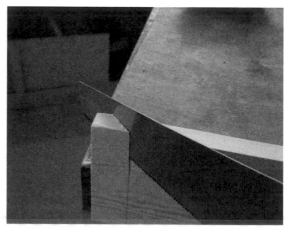

7 MARK the front and back faces as well as the 45–degree angle. This will help to keep you on track as you make the cut.

8 A sharp saw is essential for this operation. Keep your arm and elbow in line with the saw and stand so that the line on the top appears to be a continuation of the line across the face. Think of the two lines as one and begin your cut. Work slowly at first with short strokes, allowing the saw blade to run off your thumb. When the cut is established, take longer strokes and twist your wrist to guide the cut gently back on track if you find things going off–line.

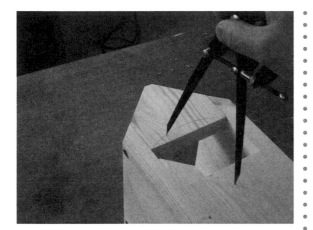

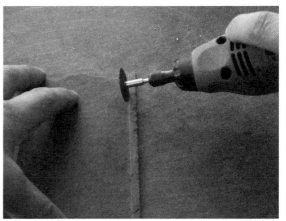

9 To increase further the size of the opening, use a pair of dividers or a round vessel to draw an arch on the top of the front section. Cut this out on a band–saw or with a jigsaw before fixing it in place with screws as before.

10 THERE are a number of ways in which you can cut the slate for the roof. A metal hacksaw will work so long as the tile is well supported beneath. A professional roofer would use snips designed for the job or even a small grinder. A Dremel with the appropriate cutter is quite adequate. HSS drill bits can be used to drill the holes for fixing. Make these slightly larger than the screws.

12 THE silicone acts like a rubber washer, as over-tightening of the screws could cause the tile to break. Finish the roof off with a piece of corner edge moulding held in place with the silicone adhesive that is available from larger DIY stores and timber yards.

11 USE a bead of silicone adhesive to act as a cushion between the tile and the timber. Tighten the screws until the adhesive just begins to squeeze out.

Hole-fronted birdhouse

This project requires cutting angles and shaping edges; it makes excellent use of rough–sawn timber off–cuts, with some leftover flooring tiles used for the roof.

THE timber used is cedar, which resists infestation from mites and other parasites that can be a problem to birds. The method of construction is simple and incorporates a door for easy cleaning of the box at the end of the breeding season. Suitable rough–sawn timber can generally be bought from a timber yard or builders' merchants in widths from 4in up to 8in (100–205mm). This house is made from 6in–wide (150mm) boards, but could easily be adapted to whatever materials are available and to suit a number of different species.

Species to expect

A house of this size with a small entrance hole of 1⅛in or 1¼in (28mm or 32mm) might attract:

UK species – house sparrow, tree sparrow, tits (blue tit, right), wren, nuthatch, pied flycatcher.

US species – nuthatch, titmouse, wren, warbler, chickadee.

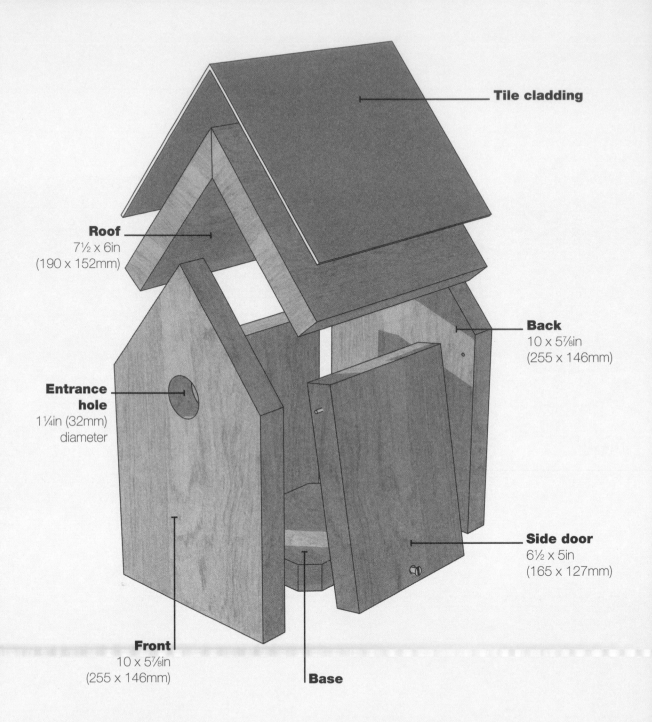

Tile cladding

Roof
7½ x 6in
(190 x 152mm)

Back
10 x 5⅞in
(255 x 146mm)

Entrance hole
1¼in (32mm)
diameter

Side door
6½ x 5in
(165 x 127mm)

Front
10 x 5⅞in
(255 x 146mm)

Base

Materials needed

Rough-sawn cedar at least ⅝in (15mm) thick
Self-adhesive floor tiles

Cutting list

Front and back 10 x 5⅞in (255 x 146mm)
Sides 6½ x 5in (165 x 127mm)
Base to suit
Roof 7½ x 6in and trim (190 x 152mm)

Box-building tip

Rough-sawn timber has a coarse texture that helps to give hatchlings a foothold up to the entrance hole when they leave the nest. Prepared or smooth timber will need roughing with a few saw-cuts to make the climb out a little easier.

1 As off-cuts and rough-sawn timber can sometimes be of unequal thickness, it is a good idea to cut the sides and the front and back pieces first. Assemble them loosely on top of the piece that will be used for the base and mark the shape to suit. To make things easier later, mark the components as they will be located when assembled.

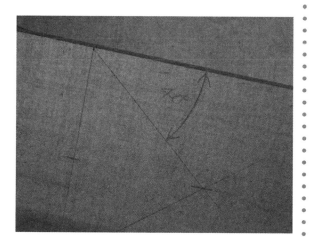

2 To cut the angle of the roof on the front and back components, use a sliding bevel set to 40 degrees and mark a line from the edge in line with the centre line for the opening.

3 Drill the hole for the opening before cutting the front to size, as larger pieces are easier to clamp or hold down. A 1¼in (32mm) hole-saw was used in a pillar drill on this occasion, but you can choose a different hole size to attract different birds (see table on page 37).

4 IT is not important for the sides to make a perfect fit to the roof. In fact, a slight gap is a good idea, as this will create necessary ventilation. The front and back are screwed to the sides. These holes can all be marked out and drilled at the same time. Note that on one side holes are drilled only at the top. This will be the side that opens as a door, and it is important that these holes are in exactly the same position on the front and back.

5 As well as ventilation, birdhouses also require a means of drainage at the bottom, as any water left to gather on the floor will increase the likelihood of disease and the decay of the birdhouse itself. The easiest way of providing this drainage is to remove the corners of the base board before assembly.

6 SCREW the house tightly together, then gradually loosen off the screws that allow the door to pivot. Fix one additional screw at the bottom of the side directly into the base, and the house is almost complete.

7 THE roof components are cut over-size and require some trimming of the edges. First, hold one of the roof pieces in place and extend the angle of the front across the edge of the roof piece. This edge can now be planed to fit. Once fixed in place, repeat this step with the other roof piece.

8 ADJUST the roof pieces to match by marking off from the other side.

9 ONCE complete, fix the roof pieces in place with screws.

10 COVER the roof with faux-slate flooring tiles to finish.

White-washed birdhouse

This little bird box is made out of ⅝in (15mm) exterior–grade plywood and some off–cuts of softwood tongue and groove. The roof uses up some leftover strips of roofing felt.

THIS design can be adapted to make different types of nest box to attract different kinds of birds – a hole–fronted box for smaller birds, such as tits or sparrows, or an open–fronted design for robins or flycatchers, for instance. The opening roof in the hole–fronted box design enables you to clean out the box thoroughly in the winter to reduce the chances of disease or infestation, but do not be tempted to inspect the box during nesting through spring and summer. The hook on the roof protects the young from predators such as crows, squirrels or rats.

Species to expect

This birdhouse would make an ideal home for:

UK species – with hole front: house sparrow, tree sparrow, tits (willow tit, right), wren, nuthatch, pied flycatcher; with open front: robin, wren, pied wagtail, spotted flycatcher.

US species – with hole front: nuthatch, titmouse, wren, warbler, chickadee, warblers; with open front: barn swallow, phoebe.

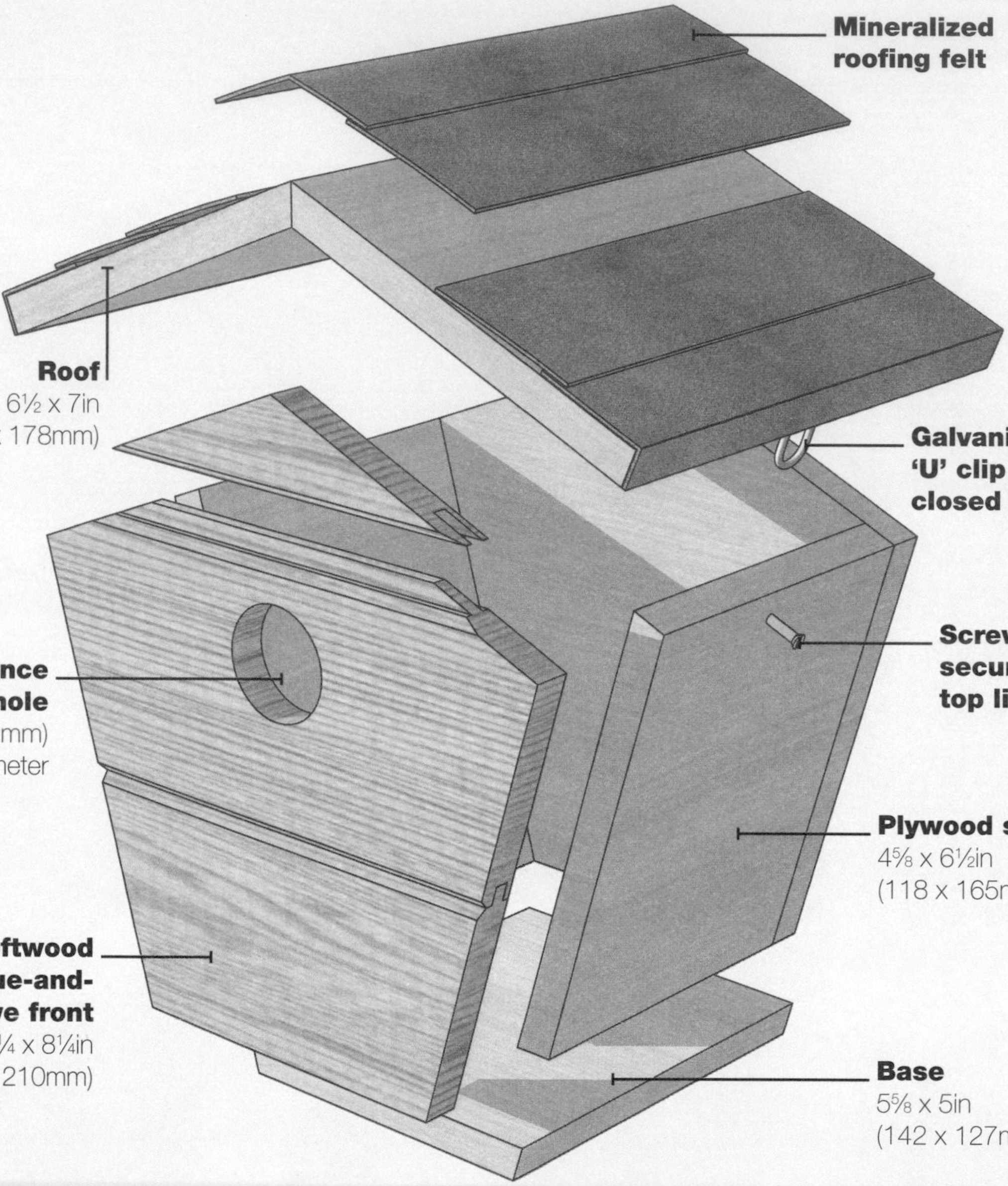

Mineralized roofing felt

Roof
6½ x 7in
(165 x 178mm)

Galvanized 'U' clip or closed hook

Entrance hole
1¼in (32mm) diameter

Screw for securing top lid

Plywood sides
4⅝ x 6½in
(118 x 165mm)

Softwood tongue-and-groove front
8¼ x 8¼in
(210 x 210mm)

Base
5⅝ x 5in
(142 x 127mm)

Materials needed

⅝in (15mm) external plywood
⅝in (15mm) softwood tongue and groove
Mineralized roofing felt
Brass hook
Polyurethane glue

Cutting list

Front and back 9 x 9in and trim (228 x 228mm)
Sides 4⅝ x 6½in and trim (118 x 165mm)
Base 5⅝ x 5in and trim (142 x 127mm)
Roof 6½ x 7in and trim (165 x 178mm)
Top 9 x 8¼in (228 x 210mm)

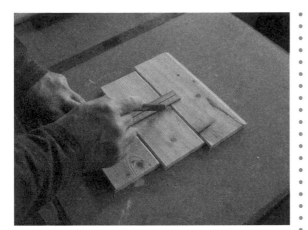

1 LINE up your pieces of tongue and groove for the front and carefully mark a centre line down the middle.

2 IF you are using very small pieces you might want to adjust the angle slightly, but don't reduce the floor size too much. Cut the angles on the individual components and use the centre line and a straight edge to make sure everything lines up.

3 WITH a closed–front box, you should provide some footholds on the interior to aid young birds in reaching the entrance hole. Some grooves like this would be fine; alternatively, glue some small strips of wood up to the hole.

4 NAIL and glue together the lower part of the box, using the front as a template for the back. Create the angles for the roof and fix one half in place with glue and pins.

5 DRILL the entrance hole 1¼in (32mm) in diameter and trim the edges of the bottom so that they match the slope of the sides.

6 REMOVE any sharp edges or splinters around the hole inside and out with some 150 grit abrasion paper.

7 DRILL a couple of small holes in the bottom of the box to allow any water that might collect inside the box to drain out.

Box-building variation

This small box is also an ideal size for birds that prefer an open-front box in which to nest (see pages 40–45 for a basic open-front birdhouse design). Follow these instructions, but assemble the front without the middle section. Obviously, there would be no need to hinge one side of the roof with this alternative design.

8 USING a craft knife, cut some strips of roofing felt 2½in (63mm) wide to lay across the top.

9 START at the base of the roof. With the loose roof piece in place, glue the strips of felt in place using either silicone adhesive or hot–melt glue. Allow an overlap of at least ½in (13mm) on each strip. The last strip to be glued along the ridge acts as a hinge, allowing the loose part of the roof to be lifted so you have access to clean out the box.

10 A closed hook fitted to the underside of the roof can be used to fix the lid closed and keep out predators.

Multiple-chamber birdhouse

There are some species of birds that are quite happy to share the same nesting box provided that each family has its own separate chamber.

This birdhouse is more of a maternity wing than a box really, and could just as well be made without the partitions and with much larger access holes to house large birds such as kestrels. The most common species of bird to use communal nesting boxes is the UK house sparrow. It is usually quite happy to seek out a suitable spot beneath the eaves of domestic buildings. This terrace–style box is an ideal alternative. Site the box high up (in the eaves), facing a direction between north and east.

Species to expect

This communal nesting box might house:

UK species – house sparrow, tree sparrow (or single nests of birds such as nuthatch).

US species – may accommodate single nests of purple martins (young purple martins, right).

Softwood top
21 x 8½in
(535 x 216mm)

Butt hinge

Battens

Plywood back board
18 x 14½in
(457 x 368mm)

Entrance hole
1¼in (32mm) diameter

Softwood ship lap front pieces x 3
18 x 4¾in
(457 x 120mm)

Plywood divider
5⅞ x 14½in
(146 x 368mm)

Plywood base
18 x 5⅞in
(457 x 146mm)

Softwood sides
7 x 14½in
(178 x 368mm)

Materials needed

⅝in (15mm) external plywood
¾in (19mm) softwood
½ x 4¾in (13 x 120mm) softwood ship lap
1 pair of 3in (76mm) galvanized hinges

Cutting list

Back (⅝in/15mm plywood) 18 x 14½in
   (457 x 368mm)
Sides 7 x 14½in (178 x 368mm)
Base (⅝in/15mm plywood) 18 x 5⅞in
   (457 x 146mm)
Top 21 x 8½in and trim (535 x 216mm)
Front 18in (457mm) lengths of 4¾in (120mm)
   softwood shiplap
Battens ¾ x ¾in (19 x 19mm)

1 TAKE the two sides that have been cut to size and use a piece of the shiplap to mark a line equal to its thickness away from the front edge.

2 USING a piece of the ⅝in (15mm) plywood, do the same to mark a line along the inside edge of the side along the bottom. These lines are used to locate the battens that will hold the front and back sections in place.

3 HOLDING one of the battens against these lines, mark off at the top to determine the correct length of the batten. Continue with this process to locate the positions for the rest of the battens and screw them into place.

4 IF you are making a terrace-style box, drill an appropriate size hole (of 1¼in, 32mm) in one of the sides.

5 HOLD the front pieces in place and then mark out a second hole position at the same height as the first.

6 PRE–DRILL the ply and pilot holes in the battens and then screw the back to the sides directly onto the battens.

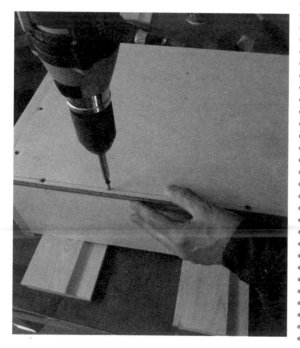

7 NOW fit the bottom in place.

8 LAY the pieces of ship lap on the front and mark out to drill for the screw holes.

9 START fixing at the top and insert the next layer before finally fixing the one before.

10 AT this point you will need to shave a little off the back at the top to line up with the angle of the sides. This is the point at which you need to insert the partitions depending on where you have placed the holes. Try to achieve two similar-sized areas.

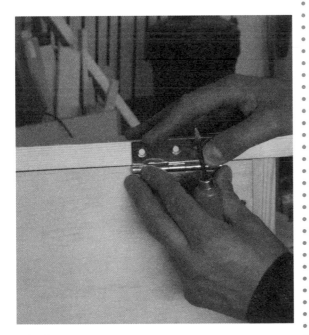

11 HOLD the hinges in place and mark the screw holes with a bradawl. It is likely that the screws will protrude into the box. You can remove them and cut them back with a hacksaw or put a second piece of timber inside the box to screw into.

12 PUT two screws through the lid into the side to keep the inhabitants safe from predators.

chalet-style birdhouse

This project is made entirely out of exterior-grade plywood. As there are exposed edges, the birdhouse will require a finish to the outer faces to protect it.

This bird box is quite large and will therefore be unsuitable for the small species of birds such as tits, sparrows or warblers. Instead the larger dimensions and hole size (1¾in, 45mm) will be preferred by starlings, flycatchers and possibly small woodpeckers. Alternatively, you could drill smaller holes in the sides and fit a partition wall inside to attract house sparrows. This design takes up quite a bit of material so it is unlikely to come out of off-cuts. You will need approximately a quarter of a sheet of ⅝in (15mm) sheet material.

Species to expect

This birdhouse might be used by:

UK species – starling.

US species – starling, bluebird (right), tree swallow, hairy woodpecker, yellow-bellied sapsucker, Carolina wren, flycatchers.

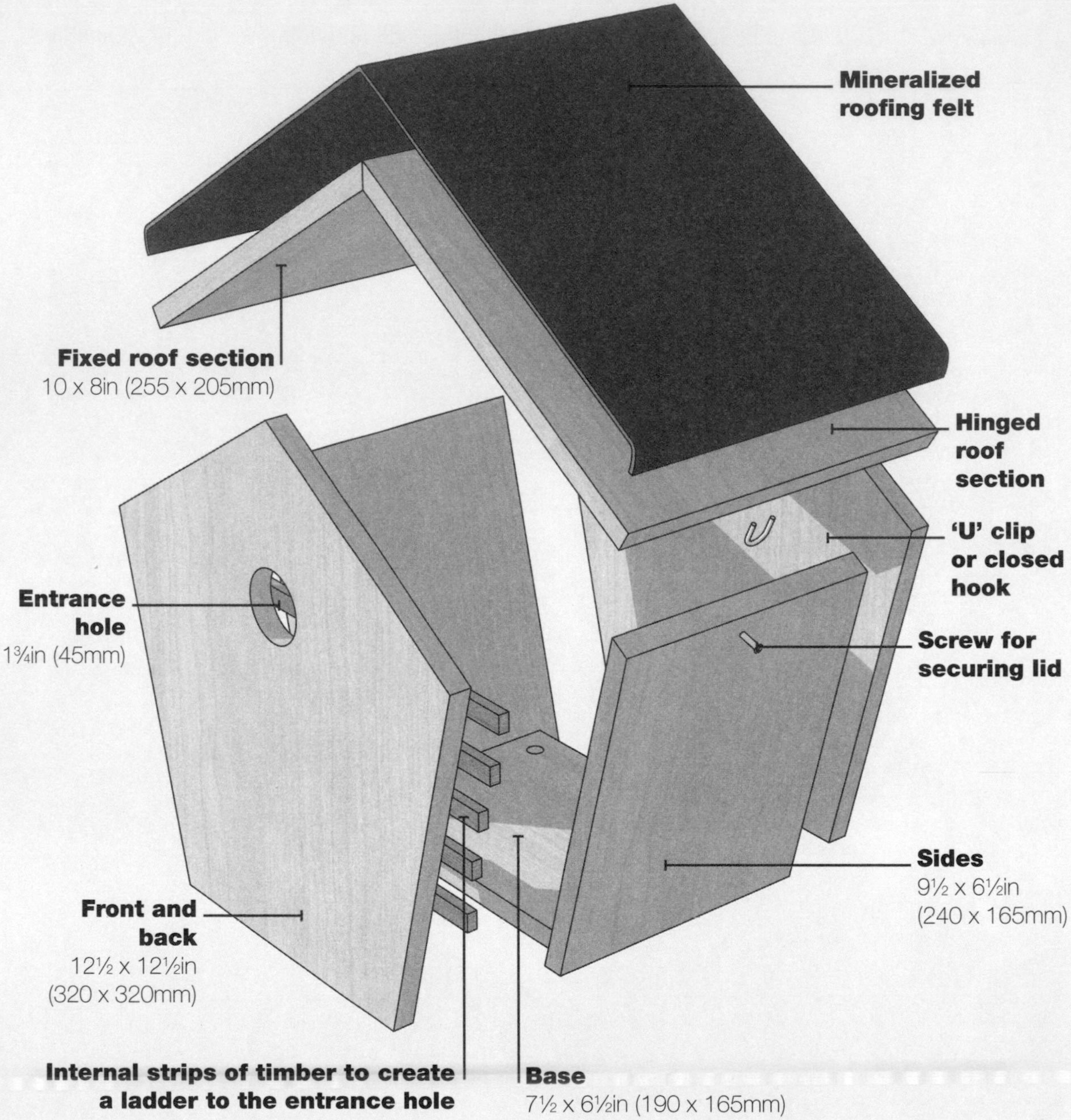

Mineralized roofing felt

Fixed roof section
10 x 8in (255 x 205mm)

Hinged roof section

'U' clip or closed hook

Entrance hole
1¾in (45mm)

Screw for securing lid

Front and back
12½ x 12½in
(320 x 320mm)

Sides
9½ x 6½in
(240 x 165mm)

Internal strips of timber to create a ladder to the entrance hole

Base
7½ x 6½in (190 x 165mm)

Materials needed

⅝in (15mm) external plywood
Roofing felt
Hook-and-eye catch
Polyurethane glue

Cutting list

Front and back 12½ x 12½in and trim
    (320 x 320mm)
Sides 9½ x 6½in and trim (240 x 165mm)
Base 7½ x 6½in (190 x 165mm)
Roof 10 x 8in and trim (255 x 205mm)

1 To get the most out of the material, it is a good idea to produce a template for the front and back pieces. You may wish to make a slightly smaller template to make a smaller box out of the off–cuts.

2 A fine-tooth panel saw will achieve a cleaner cut if you are unable to use a machine.

3 The crucial components are the front and back, so take a little time to get these identical and symmetrical. Accurate measurements for the other components will come from these two pieces.

4 When you are satisfied that everything fits without any gaps, glue and pin the bottom half of the box together.

5 POLYURETHANE glue is an excellent exterior-grade adhesive and is widely available. It will foam and expand to fill small gaps, but will need to be cleaned from the faces on the inside of the box.

6 DRILL the entrance hole 1¾in (45mm) in diameter. This size is suitable for starlings and flycatcher amongst others (see page 64).

7 PREPARE to fit the roof, making sure the mitres meet neatly across the top. Glue and pin only one side of the roof.

8 On the inside of the box, supply a means to help young birds make their way to the entrance hole. This could consist of simple grooves cut into the surface, but we have made a series of footholds from small sticks. Drill a hole of ⅜in (9mm) in each corner of the bottom of the box to allow any water to drain away.

9 Apply the finish to the outside of the box and fix the felt to the roof with the loose section in place.

10 An improvised hook and eye will keep the lid closed to protect the birds from predators.

Box-building variation

This box could just as easily be made from pieces of solid timber and screwed together – avoiding the need for a finish altogether. Rubber matting would make a good alternative to roofing felt.

Domed birdhouse

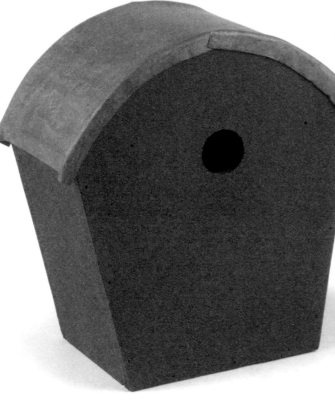

This simple but attractive nest box design, with its curved roof, is relatively easy to build and uses cheap, easy–to–find plywood and lead sheet for the roof to protect the inhabitants.

THIS medium–sized bird box is suitable – with a hole size of 1¾in (45mm) or more – for the larger common garden birds, such as starlings in the UK or the bluebird and various woodpecker, flycatcher and finch species in the US. If you decide to treat your box with preservative to lengthen its lifespan, remember to use only a water–based preservative, safe for birds, and only apply it to the outside of the box, and not to the inside or around the entrance hole.

Species to expect

This medium-sized bird box might attract:

UK species – starling.

US species – starling, bluebird, tree swallow (right), hairy woodpecker, yellow-bellied sapsucker, Carolina wren, flycatchers.

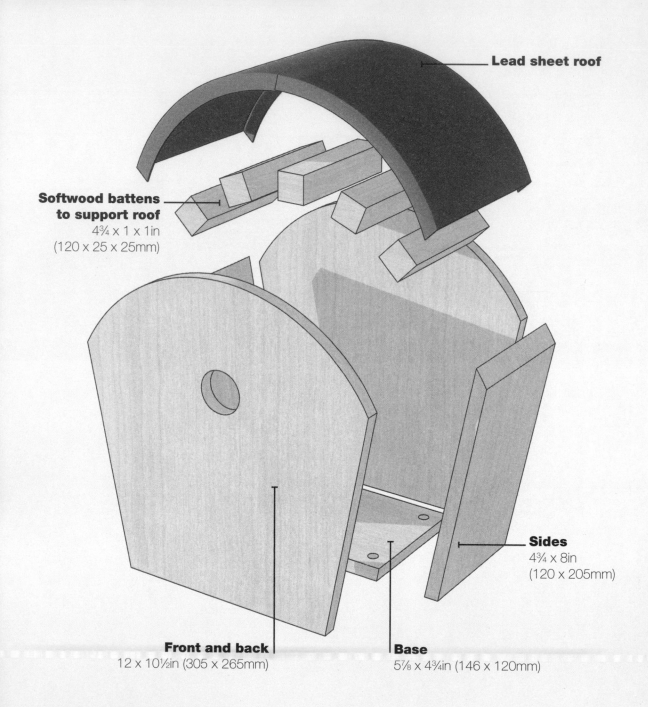

Lead sheet roof

**Softwood battens
to support roof**
4¾ x 1 x 1in
(120 x 25 x 25mm)

Front and back
12 x 10½in (305 x 265mm)

Base
5⅞ x 4¾in (146 x 120mm)

Sides
4¾ x 8in
(120 x 205mm)

Materials needed

⅝in (15mm) external plywood
Lead sheeting offcut approximately
    ¹⁄₁₆in (1.5mm) thick
Softwood batten 1 x 1in (25 x 25mm)

Cutting list

Front and back 12 x 10½in and trim
    (305 x 265mm)
Sides 4¾ x 8in (120 x 205mm)
Base 5⅞ x 4¾in (146 x 120mm)
Battens 4¾ x 1 x 1in (120 x 25 x 25mm)

Box-building tip

Bird boxes that are finished in a dark colour and have a metal roof like this one should never be placed where they will be exposed to direct sunlight at the warmest part of the day. This is good advice for all nesting boxes, since birds tend to cope better compensating for extreme cold rather than heat.

1 MARK out and draw the shape for the front and back pieces on one of the components.

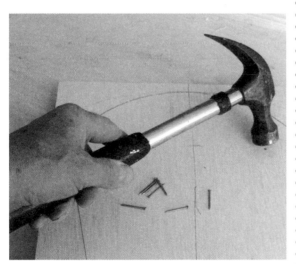

2 USING some small pins, fix the two components together firmly but not so firmly that you cannot separate them later.

3 USING either a band–saw or jigsaw, cut the two components out at the same time.

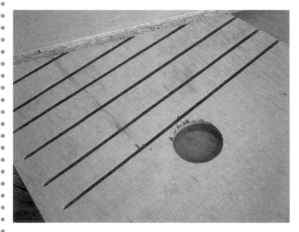

4 SEPARATE the pieces and drill the appropriate hole for the species you have in mind (see page 37 for more details).

5 CREATE some grooves on the inside of the front piece below the entrance hole to create footholds for young birds.

7 TAKE a length of the batten and mark it to cut to length to fit between the front and back.

6 GLUE and pin the front, back and sides together. Drill some small holes in the base of the box to allow any water that may get trapped inside to drain away.

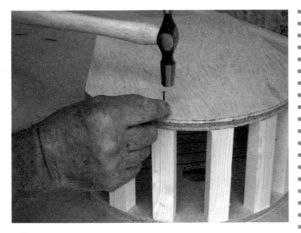

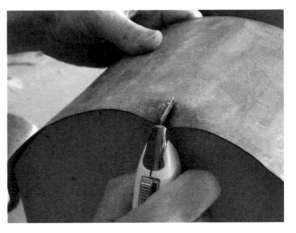

8 Fix the battens in place with pins and glue except for one. This will need to be fixed with screws so that it can be removed in the future to enable you to clean the box out.

9 Thin–gauge lead can be cut with a craft knife. Prepare a strip about 1in (25mm) wider than the depth of the box. Lay it on the top and gently press it into shape, removing a small V–shape at the top of the curve, front and back.

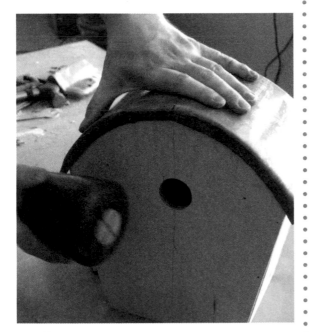

10 With a mallet, gently dress the lead over the edge of the box. Be careful not to over–work it, as this could tear the material.

Box-building variation

In an area where extremely low night-time temperatures are expected, it would be advisable to incorporate a layer of insulation within the roof space of the box.

Bat houses

simple slatted bat house

This bat box makes use of rough-sawn timber that is an ideal material for the job. The texture allows much-needed grip for the inhabitants to cling to when entering and leaving the box.

Bats can be quite choosy about the state of their residence so, although the timber used in its construction may be rough, the box itself needs to be fitted together without too many gaps. Take care to make sure the corresponding angles of the sides are all the same. The front is made so that it can be opened easily. This is not to be used to gain a glimpse of the bats when they are nesting, but to facilitate the fixing of the box through the back board. Do not use wood preservatives, since the chemicals can harm or kill bats.

Species to expect

This bat box might become home to:

UK species – common pipistrelle, Natterer's bat, brown long-eared bat, Leisler's bat, noctule, Daubenton's bat, Bechstein's bat, barbastelle.

US species – eastern pipistrelle, little brown bat, big brown bat, evening bat, Mexican free-tailed bat, Pallas's mastiff bat (right), long-eared bat, south-eastern bat, pallid bat.

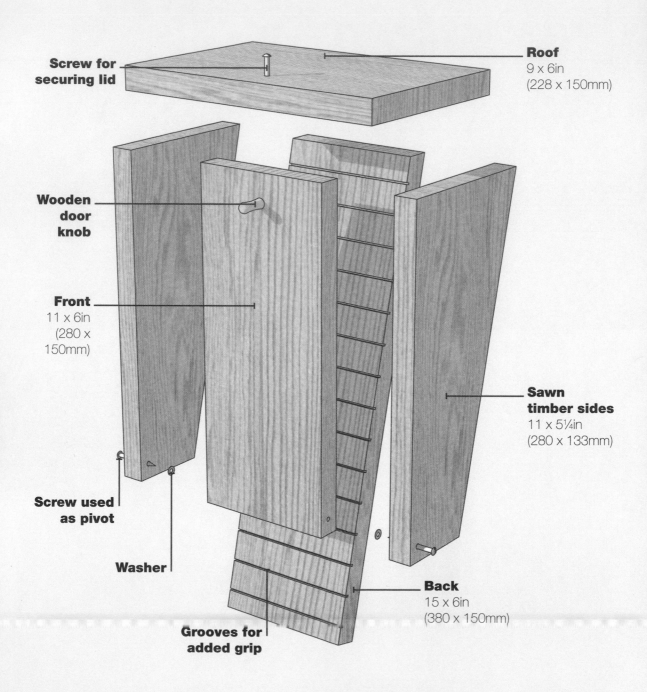

Roof
9 x 6in
(228 x 150mm)

**Screw for
securing lid**

**Wooden
door
knob**

Front
11 x 6in
(280 x
150mm)

**Sawn
timber sides**
11 x 5¼in
(280 x 133mm)

**Screw used
as pivot**

Washer

Back
15 x 6in
(380 x 150mm)

**Grooves for
added grip**

Materials needed

Rough-sawn timber
Door knob
Pivot screws

Cutting list

Back 15 x 6in (380 x 150mm)
Front 11 x 6in (280 x 150mm)
Sides 11 x 5¼in (280 x 133mm) cut to suit
Roof 9 x 6in (228 x 150mm)

1 MARK out and cut the side components as per the diagram opposite. Use one completed side as a template for the second side, or produce a template from a thin sheet of plywood or MDF if you intend to make more than one box.

2 THERE is a slight angle on the top of the back board. To mark this before cutting, offer up a side component or your template to the edge and make a mark. If you are cutting by hand, repeat this on the other edge and extend the lines to show a continuous line around the back board. It is a good idea to make the back board longer than required just in case you need more than one attempt at this.

3 ON the inside of the back board, you will need to create some grooves for the bats to hang from. Using a square, mark these out from the bottom at 1in (25mm) intervals to within 2 or 3in (50–76mm) of the top.

4 THE grooves can be cut using a cross–cut saw with a trenching facility set to a depth of ³⁄₁₆in (5mm).

5 ALTERNATIVELY, you could use a handsaw. A fine–tooth saw might need to make two cuts ⅛in (3mm) apart to form a V–shape.

6 BEGIN assembly by fixing the sides onto the back with some screws.

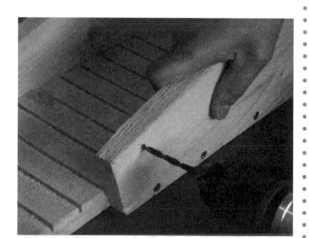

7 PRE–DRILL the holes for the pivot screws in the sides that will fasten to the front.

8 FIX a knob or some similar device to the front of the door.

9 POKE the pivot screws through the holes and place a washer on each of them.

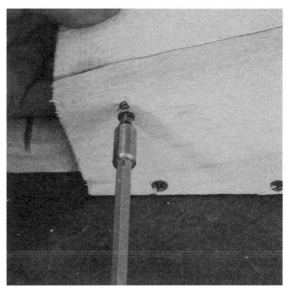

10 WITH the door held in place, tighten the screw but not so tightly that the door is stiff to open.

11 FIX the lid to the top of the box, leaving one screw that will fix the door in place when it is hung.

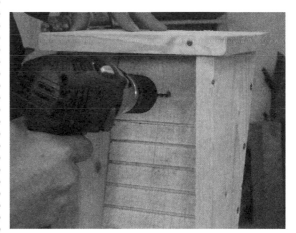

12 DRILL the final holes in the back for fixing the box in place.

Single-slot bat house

This bat box design makes use of materials that are easily obtained from a well–stocked timber yard or builders' merchants.

Most of the components for this bat house are cut from a sheet of 1 x 9in (25 x 228mm) prepared softwood timber, with a finished dimension of ¾ x 8½in (19 x 216mm). The front is made up from ship lap cladding, of the sort often used to face the exterior of buildings. The design provides a ventilation slot to prevent any animals roosting inside from overheating in hot weather. Remember to cut grooves into the panels to help the bats grip the surfaces when they land and roost.

Species to expect

This bat house might offer shelter to:

UK species – common pipistrelle, Natterer's bat, brown long-eared bat, Leisler's bat, noctule, Daubenton's bat, Bechstein's bat, barbastelle.

US species – eastern pipistrelle, little brown bat (right), big brown bat, evening bat, Mexican free-tailed bat, Pallas's mastiff bat, long-eared bat, south-eastern bat, pallid bat.

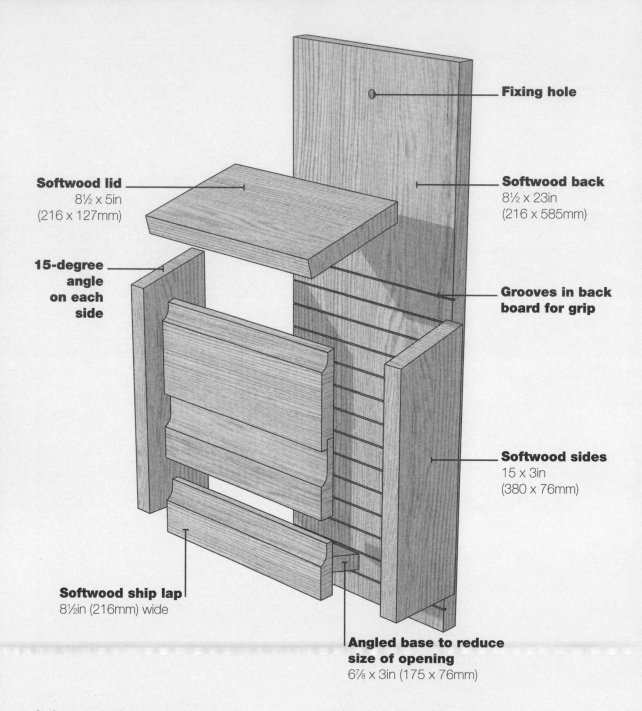

Fixing hole

Softwood lid
8½ x 5in
(216 x 127mm)

Softwood back
8½ x 23in
(216 x 585mm)

15-degree
angle
on each
side

Grooves in back
board for grip

Softwood sides
15 x 3in
(380 x 76mm)

Softwood ship lap
8½in (216mm) wide

Angled base to reduce
size of opening
6⅞ x 3in (175 x 76mm)

Materials needed

¾in (19mm) prepared softwood
5in (127mm) softwood ship lap
   (4¾in/120mm finished)
Silicone sealant

Cutting list

Back 8½ x 23in (216 x 585mm)
Lid 8½ x 5in and trim (216 x 127mm)
Sides 15 x 3in and trim (380 x 76mm)
Base 6⅞ x 3in and trim (175 x 76mm)
Ship lap 8½in (216mm)

1 HAVING cut your ship lap to size, remove the lip on two of the pieces and leave one piece untouched for now.

2 HAVING cut your side pieces with a 15-degree angle on one end, use this to mark the same angle on the edge of one of the ship lap pieces at the thin edge. Using a plane, create this angle along the top (thin) edge. This will become the top section of the front of the box.

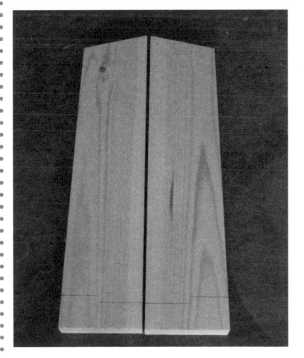

3 TAKE the piece you have cut for the lid and follow the same process to create a 15-degree bevel along one long edge. Then do exactly the same to the two long edges for the bottom piece.

4 ON one side, hold the bottom in place so that the angled edge is flush with the front edge of the side. Make some marks where you think the screws need to be to hold the bottom in place. Lay the sides back to back then front to front to replicate these lines on the other side.

5 REPEAT this process to establish precisely where you need to drill the holes for the screws. The bottom of this box is sloped to help bat droppings fall out, and the gap is large enough for it to be used as an entrance hole.

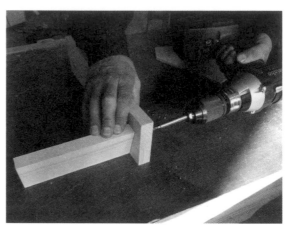

6 TAKE one side and hold it firmly face down on the bench with the bottom in place. Now screw together.

7 WITH the sides and bottom screwed together, hold them on the face of the back board and draw round the inside, top and bottom.

8 IF you make this box from smooth-faced timber or ply, you will need to create some form of grip for the bats to cling onto when they are inside. Here, I have cut some grooves using a cross-cut saw to within a couple of inches (about 50mm) from the top of the box.

9 MARK two lines across the back where the lid will go and then drill holes at an angle for the screws. A quick and easy way to do this is to hold the side with the correct angle close to where you are drilling and line it up by eye.

10 DRILL holes in the back and fix to the sides. Take the first piece of ship lap (with the angle on the top edge) and fix it in place with two screws at the top. Slide the second piece underneath the lip and hold it in place while you put the second screws in. The last piece of ship lap is fixed with the bottom edge flush with the bottom of the sides.

11 To help make this box as warm and dry as possible, use a line of silicone sealant around the edges where the lid will fit.

12 FINALLY, screw the lid on. Once the box is assembled, you may wish to run a second bead of silicone along the top edge on the outside. If you have even the slightest gap now it will only increase as the timber begins to acclimatize to being out in all weathers.

Two-tiered bat house

This box makes use of small lengths of tongue–and–groove board that you may have left over from another project. Alternatively, it is widely available from DIY stores, builders' merchants and timber yards.

THIS design of bat box provides two interior cavities that resemble natural crevices, and is particularly attractive to some small bat species. It is also large enough to house a number of bats and would be a good choice for a location that is already in the vicinity of an established bat community. Consider providing more than one bat box, each one facing in a different direction, to provide the bats with a choice of roosting place as the weather and the position of the sun change.

Species to expect

This bat box might become inhabited by:

UK species – common pipistrelle, Natterer's bat, brown long-eared bat, Leisler's bat, noctule, Daubenton's bat, Bechstein's bat, barbastelle.

US species – eastern pipistrelle, little brown bat, big brown bat, evening bat, Mexican free-tailed bat, Pallas's mastiff bat, long-eared bat (right), south-eastern bat, pallid bat.

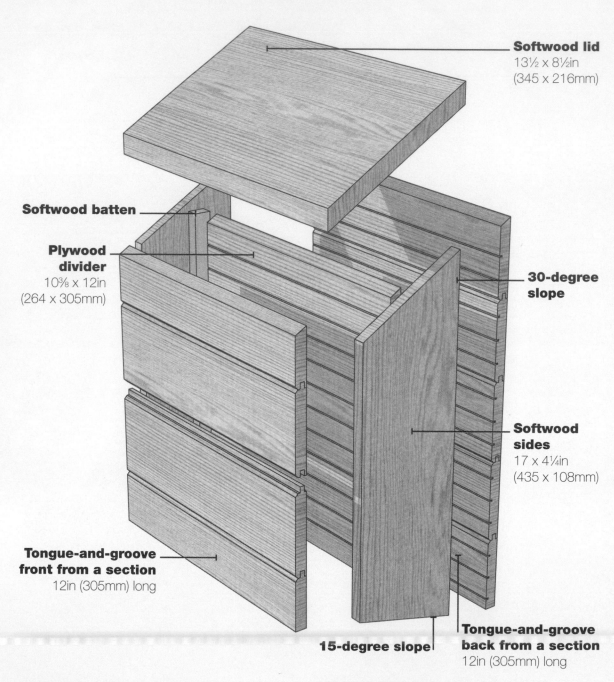

Softwood lid
13½ x 8½in
(345 x 216mm)

Softwood batten

Plywood divider
10⅜ x 12in
(264 x 305mm)

30-degree slope

Softwood sides
17 x 4¼in
(435 x 108mm)

Tongue-and-groove front from a section
12in (305mm) long

15-degree slope

Tongue-and-groove back from a section
12in (305mm) long

Materials needed

¾in (19mm) prepared softwood timber
3½ x ½in softwood tongue and groove
(90 x 13mm)
Silicone adhesive

Cutting list

Front and back 9 x 12in-long (305mm)
tongue-and-groove boards
Lid 13½ x 8½in and trim (345 x 216mm)
Sides 17 x 4¼in and trim (435 x 108mm)
Divider 10⅜ x 12in (264 x 305mm)
Battens 1 x ¾ x 12in (25 x 19 x 305mm)

1 START by cutting the back and side pieces and lay them out as they will be in the finished project. Number the back panels 1 to 5. Mark out the grooves that will be needed to give the bats something to grip onto on the inside of the box.

2 MARK a centre line down the middle of both of the sides on the inside face.

3 PLACE the sides together back to back, and square off a line to represent the length of the battens that will be used to fix the central divider in place. It is not critical, but leave a gap of around 1in (25mm) at the top.

4 SCREW the battens in place towards the back edge and slightly away from the centre line, by about half the thickness of the central divider.

5 TAKE the first of the back pieces and cut the tongue off. Plane or cut a 30–degree angle to match the side and fix in place with one screw for the time being.

6 PLACE the rest of the back pieces in position and mark a line in from the edge to drill the holes for the rest of the screws. Do not drill anything yet.

7 MOVE to the last piece and drill a hole at an angle, roughly the same as the 15–degree angle on the bottom of the side. Put the last screw in now. As it is going in at an angle, it will help to close up the other pieces nice and tight.

8 DRILL and screw the central divider into place. Note that I have put some grooves into the ply as well.

9 As screws are not being used to fix the front panels, apply a bead of silicone adhesive before nailing the front on.

10 Turn the box upside down onto the lid and mark out with pencil where the sides meet underneath.

12 Drill two holes between the lines, run a bead of adhesive around all the edges, and screw the top on.

11 With an off-cut of the material used to make the sides, mark the inside edge of the sides to indicate clearly where you need to drill for the holes to fix the top.

Box-building tip

A sturdy back board is essential to help get a firm fixing for a bat box, which should ideally be mounted around 16½ft (5m) off the ground.

Bee houses

Wood-block bee house

This bee house makes use of some leftover oak flooring and a log that was saved from the wood burner. The size of log you choose will determine the dimensions.

NOT all bees nest in colonies; many are known as 'solitary bees' and these nest in small tunnels and holes, often excavated by beetles, where the female divides the tunnel into individual cells. You can create nesting sites for solitary bees by drilling differently sized holes in a block of wood. Position the house so it is sheltered from the weather and facing the morning sun. Although this project uses a round log, split logs are readily available and could just as easily be used.

Species to expect

This bee house might give shelter to:

UK species – leafcutter bees, mason bees, sweat bees, wool-carding bees and carpenter bees.

US species – leafcutter bees, mason bees (right), sweat bees, wool-carding bees and carpenter bees.

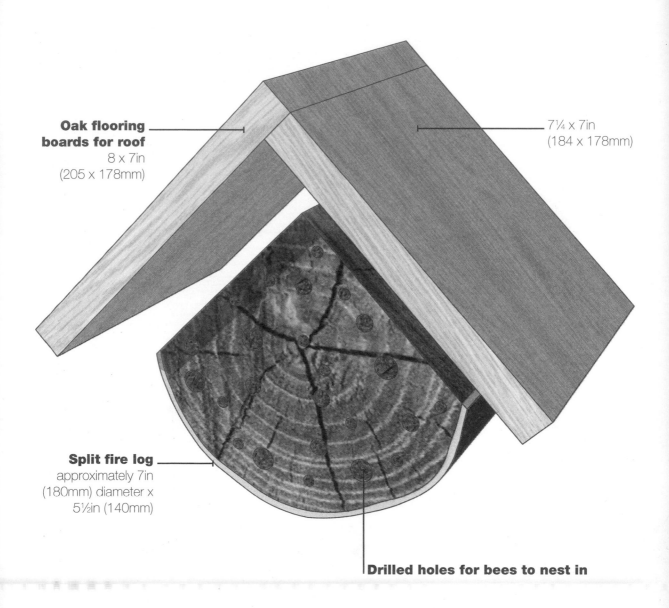

Oak flooring boards for roof
8 x 7in
(205 x 178mm)

7¼ x 7in
(184 x 178mm)

Split fire log
approximately 7in
(180mm) diameter x
5½in (140mm)

Drilled holes for bees to nest in

Materials needed

Split log
Oak flooring off-cuts
Adhesive
Galvanized nails

1 SAWING the odd log by hand can be rather satisfying providing you have a sharp saw and a steady platform to work on. Most popular timber species are suitable and need not cost the earth. I used ash for this project.

2 FALLEN and unseasoned logs can be hard work to saw, so if possible use a machine to make the cuts through the grain. Make an initial straight cut through the log.

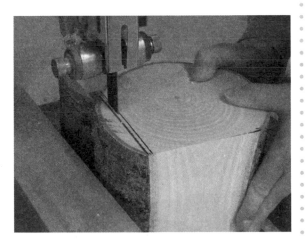

3 CREATE a second cut at right angles to the first. There are no hard and fast measurements to follow, but try not to remove too much of the log.

4 WITH a selection of drills, make a random pattern of holes going as deep as you can in the face of the log.

5 HOLES with a diameter of ¼in up to ½in (6–13mm) will be sufficient. The length of your drill bit will determine the depth.

6 MARK and cut your roof sections from the flat material. These sizes are not critical but allow for a reasonable overhang to shelter the holes from the rain.

7 USING an exterior-grade adhesive, glue the roof sections in place. Polyurethane or silicone adhesive will allow for movement over the seasons.

8 USE galvanized nails to hold things in place while the glue is drying. It will help to pre-drill the holes first.

9 FOR a neat job, make sure that things line up along the top edges. Be sure to run a line of glue where the roof sections meet.

10 A sander may be needed to finish things off. Wait for the glue to dry completely first.

Box-building variation

A large square section of timber (perhaps an off-cut from an oak beam) would work just as well – as long as it has not been treated with any chemicals.

Teardrop bee house

Bamboo canes make perfect tunnels for solitary bees to nest in, and the canes can be easily found, making this a quick and easy project.

BUNDLES of bamboo canes provide good nest sites for some species of solitary bee. Remember to position one end of this bee house against a wall, or block off the canes, to ensure the tunnels are sheltered for the insects, and hang the bee house so that the open holes face the morning sun. The overall size of this bee house can be changed to suit the number of canes that you have. The house is held together with wire; you could use string as well, but this would not allow you form the teardrop shape quite so easily.

Species to expect

This bee house might become home to:

UK species – leafcutter bees, mason bees, sweat bees, wool-carding bees and carpenter bees.

US species – leafcutter bees (right), mason bees, sweat bees, wool-carding bees and carpenter bees.

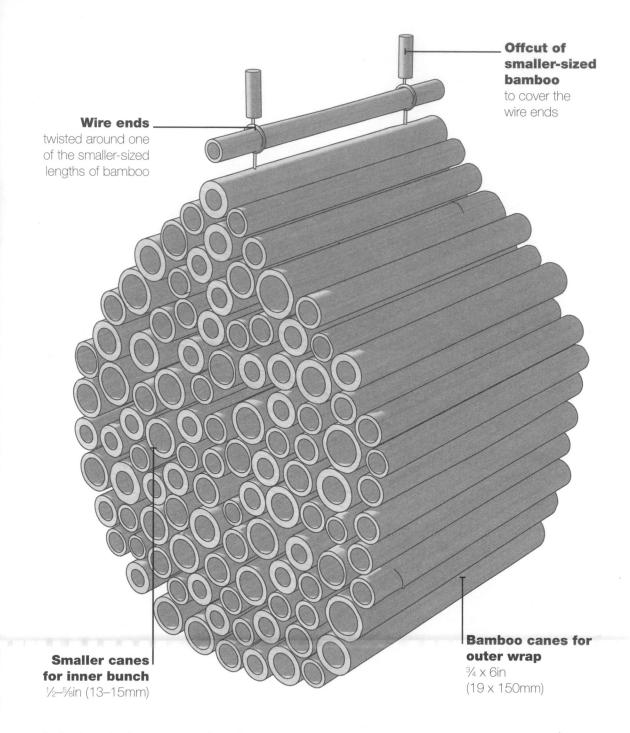

Wire ends
twisted around one of the smaller-sized lengths of bamboo

Offcut of smaller-sized bamboo
to cover the wire ends

Smaller canes for inner bunch
½–⅝in (13–15mm)

Bamboo canes for outer wrap
¾ x 6in
(19 x 150mm)

Materials needed

1⁄16in (1.5mm) wire
Assortment of bamboo canes cut to 6in (150mm)
Mitre block

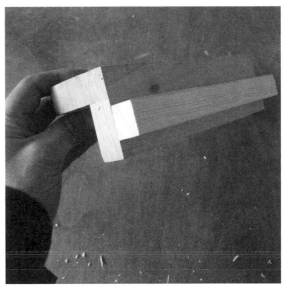

1 THIS project makes use of a wooden mitre block, which is available from most hardware shops. Clamp or screw a block of wood to the mitre block 6in (150mm) from one end. Use this as a stop to make sure all the pieces of cane are the same length. Whatever is overhanging the mitre block is waste. If cutting by hand, a fine–tooth saw makes things easier and causes less breakout.

2 FIX a second block of wood to the bottom part of the mitre block to make a cradle to rest the bamboo sections on.

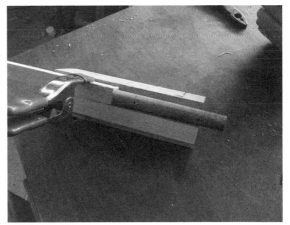

3 SELECT the canes that you intend to use for the outer layer. I used the larger size. Lay the canes in the cradle and, using a pen resting on the edge of the mitre block, run a mark along the length of each cane.

4 CLAMP a second piece of wood in place to the underneath so that the outer pieces overhang the mitre block by 1in (25mm). Make a mark at this point on the line for the hole position. Do this to both ends of the cane. This will help to make sure that the holes are in line as well as at the same distance from the ends.

5 Use the mitre block as a cradle to hold the canes for drilling and thread them onto the wires, keeping the wire as straight as possible.

6 Use a pair of pliers to give a few twists to the wire. Then insert a smaller one and repeat with a few twists on the top until the outer layer is tight.

7 Before filling the wrap with the loose canes, make sure that they are hollow by drilling out the soft core as deep as you can.

8 Having a selection of different size canes will mean that no fixing is necessary. Push them into place firmly to achieve a tight fit.

9 SOME gentle squeezing and moulding by hand will allow you to form the house into a teardrop shape that will keep its form once it is hung up.

10 TRIM the ends off the wire. They will be rather sharp after doing this, so fit a small piece of cane over the ends.

Box-building tip

Some garden centres sell pre-made edging made from bamboo and similar materials, which could be used to make this a really quick and easy project. Either roll up the edging to form a round shape or use it just for the outer layer.

Box-building variation

You could use solid wood doweling for the outer wrap layer instead of bamboo to create a visual contrast.

Bumblebee house

This is a simple house to build and is specially designed to suit certain species of bumblebee. Make sure that it is in place before the spring, when the queens will be searching for a nest site.

THE box consists of two compartments – the outer one acts as a defence and latrine area, and the inner as the nesting compartment. Bees like good ventilation in their nest, and you can ensure this by moulding some chicken wire into a bowl–like shape and placing it in the inner compartment so that there is plenty of air around it. Put a good handful of nesting material, such as dry moss, horsehair or hamster bedding from a pet shop, in the wire bowl.

Species to expect

This bumblebee house may attract:

UK species – red-tailed bumblebee, early bumblebee, buff-tailed bumblebee (right), garden bumblebee, common carder bumblebee.

US species – red-belted bumblebee, brown-belted bumblebee, yellow bumblebee, half black bumblebee.

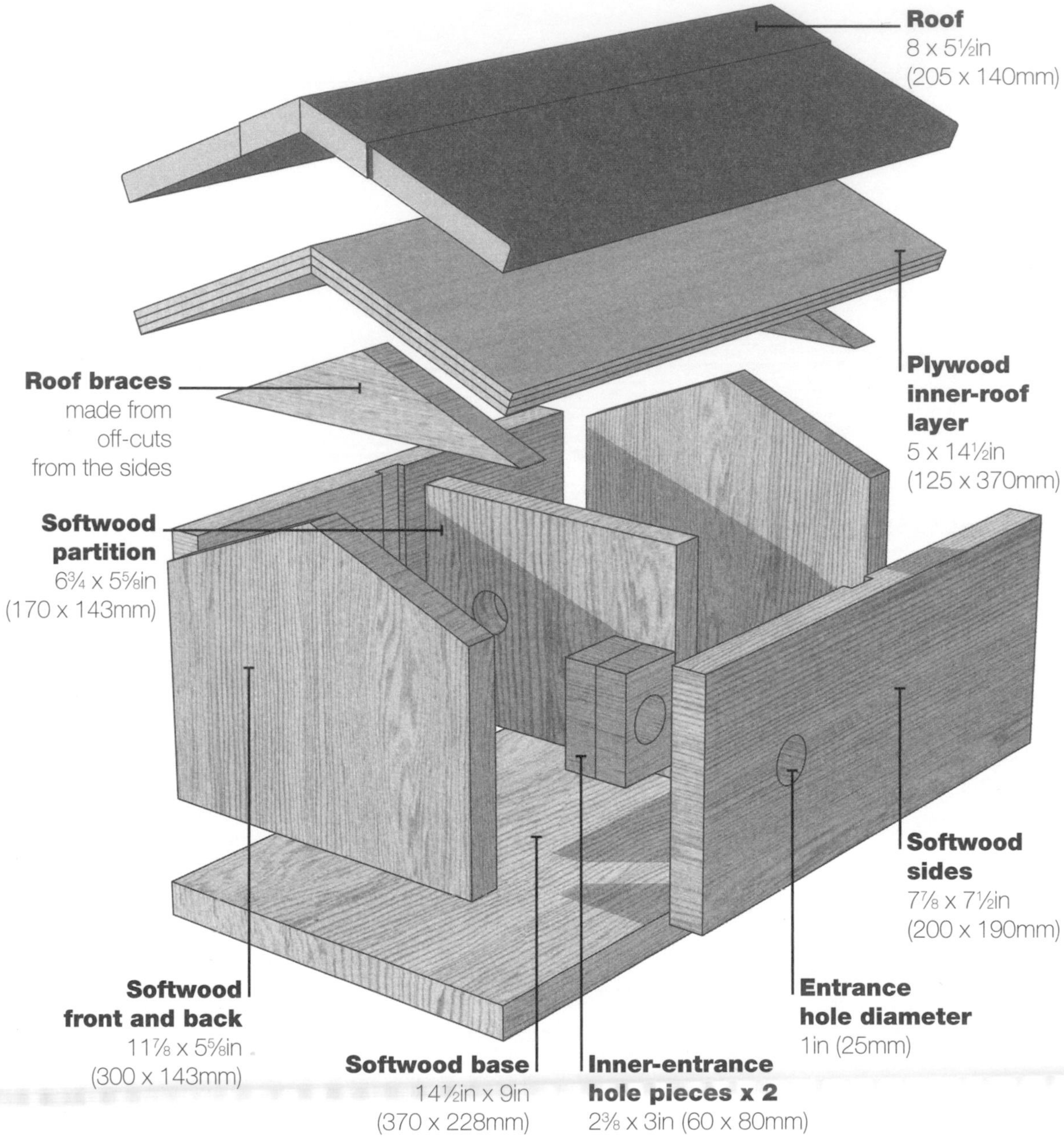

Roof
8 x 5½in
(205 x 140mm)

Roof braces
made from
off-cuts
from the sides

**Plywood
inner-roof
layer**
5 x 14½in
(125 x 370mm)

**Softwood
partition**
6¾ x 5⅝in
(170 x 143mm)

**Softwood
sides**
7⅞ x 7½in
(200 x 190mm)

**Softwood
front and back**
11⅞ x 5⅝in
(300 x 143mm)

Softwood base
14½in x 9in
(370 x 228mm)

**Inner-entrance
hole pieces x 2**
2⅜ x 3in (60 x 80mm)

**Entrance
hole diameter**
1in (25mm)

Materials needed

¾in (19mm) prepared softwood
⅝in (15mm) exterior-grade ply
Lead sheet
Silicone sealant or mastic adhesive

Cutting list

Sides 7⅞ x 7½in (200 x 190mm)
Partition 6¾ x 5⅝in (170 x 143mm)
Front and back 11⅞ x 5⅝in (300 x 143mm)
Base 14½in x 9in (370 x 228mm)
Roof 5 x 14½in (125 x 370mm)

1 FIRST prepare your components from the cutting list and butt the ends up against the front and back pieces. Make a line on the inside face of the ends at the top of the sides.

2 FROM these lines, mark out the angles of the roof from a central line at the top. Cut along these lines and keep the triangular pieces as they will be used to brace the roof.

3 TAKE a pair of these triangular off-cuts and mark them out together to drill for dowels by aligning the two sloping edges and the square ends. The flat bottom edges do not have to be even.

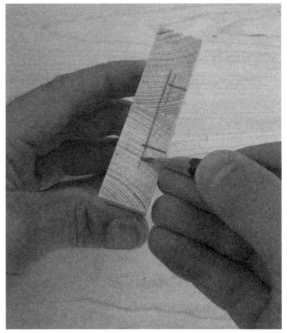

4 NOW hold the pieces together and working from the same edge, make a second mark to pinpoint the centre of the hole for the dowel.

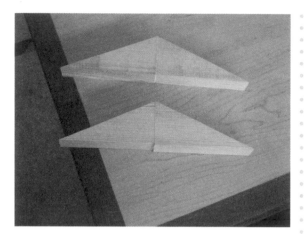

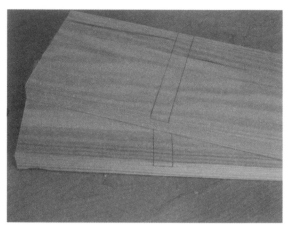

5 USING glue and a dowel, fix the two pieces together to make a single roof-shaped triangle. Do this with the other two pieces to make a pair of roof supports.

6 MARK out where the partition will be on the inside edges of the front and back pieces. As the position it is not critical, you can off-set it so that the box will only fit together one way – making any mistakes when assembling impossible.

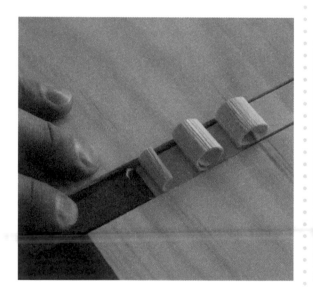

7 USE a straight edge to make saw cuts along these lines to a depth of ³⁄₁₆in (5mm) and remove the waste from one end to the middle with a chisel. Repeat from the other end.

8 THE entrance into the box is through a tunnel. Glue and screw a block of wood to the inside face of the front where you want the entrance hole to be. Dowel or screw a second block in place, making sure there is enough space to drill a 1in (25mm) diameter hole through all three pieces from the front.

9 BEFORE gluing and screwing the box together, drill a hole in the partition to allow access between the two chambers.

10 ASSEMBLE the lid using the roof braces, positioning them away from the edge so that they locate on the inside of the box when the lid is in place. You can use the join line of the braces to indicate the angle required to form the ridge along the top of the roof.

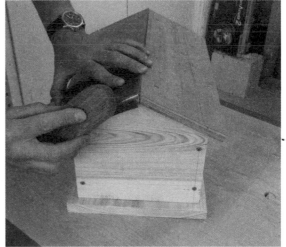

11 THE lead for the roof was laid in three sections. Use a sharp craft knife to cut the lead in a series of scores against a straight edge. To create the folds in the lead, clamp a piece of wood along the crease over the edge of your bench and work the shape with a block of wood and a hammer. Avoid the temptation to use the hammer directly on the lead since it can easily force the material out of shape.

12 WITH a similar block of wood continue to shape the lead onto the roof and secure it in place with a silicone sealant or a mastic-based adhesive. A single strip across the ridge will seal the joint.

Bug houses

simple bamboo bug house

This bug house uses some easily found natural materials, such as bamboo canes, pieces of wood, twigs and plant stems, to provide a range of homes for lots of different invertebrates.

THIS project is perfect for making with kids. Start with a search for suitable branches and twigs, and then make your bug house to suit the materials available. Materials that are sourced in the location where you intend to site your box are likely to be attractive to suitable inhabitants. A vast number of invertebrates, including spiders, ladybugs, solitary bees and beetle larvae will find the wood and plant–stem tunnels irresistible and quickly make nests or hibernate in them.

Species to expect

This bug house might become occupied by:

UK species – wood-boring beetle larvae, spiders, ladybugs (right), lacewings, solitary bee species (including leafcutter, mason, sweat, wool-carding and carpenter bees).

US species – wood-boring beetle larvae, spiders, ladybugs, lacewings, solitary bee species (including leafcutter, mason, sweat, wool-carding and carpenter bees).

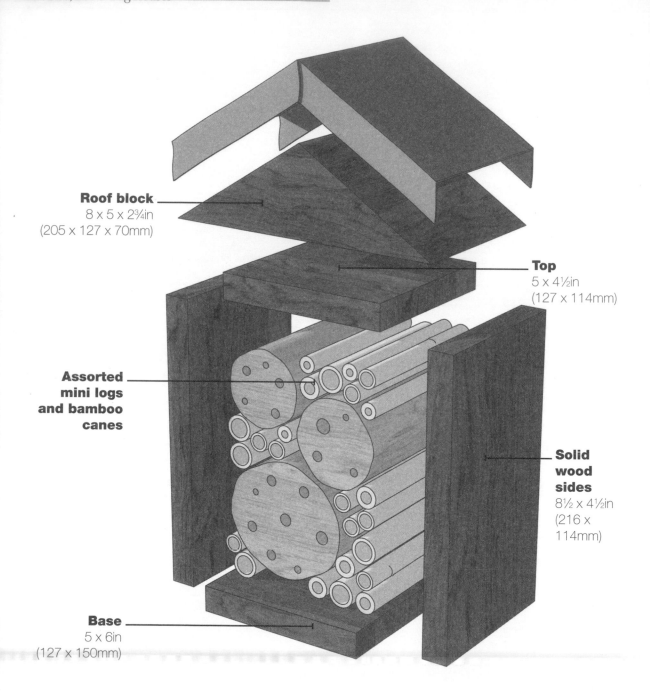

Roof block
8 x 5 x 2¾in
(205 x 127 x 70mm)

Top
5 x 4½in
(127 x 114mm)

Assorted mini logs and bamboo canes

Solid wood sides
8½ x 4½in
(216 x 114mm)

Base
5 x 6in
(127 x 150mm)

Materials needed

Softwood or hardwood timber
Mini-logs
Bamboo canes
Lead
Adhesive

Cutting list

Sides 8½ x 4½in (216 x 114mm)
Top 5 x 4½in (127 x 114mm)
Base 5 x 6in (127 x 150mm)
Roof block 8 x 5 x 2¾in (205 x 127 x 70mm)

1 MARK and cut out the components for the box frame from solid wood.

2 CHECK that everything fits together before attempting to fix together.

3 LAY the components out in a way that makes sense, and apply an external–grade adhesive to the joints. You may want to pre–drill any hardwood to make nailing a little easier.

4 A clamp or second pair of hands comes in handy to hold things in place while driving home some nails.

5 USE a fine-tooth saw to cut the lengths of bamboo to the depth of the box frame.

6 PACK the logs and the bamboo sticks tightly into the box frame. Use the sticks to wedge the mini-logs in place. Drill holes of varying sizes into the logs.

7 MARK a centre line on the roof block on the edges to create the point on the roof.

8 MARK the diagonals from one long edge to the opposite corners and cut to form the roof block.

9 GLUE and nail the roof block in place on the box frame and round over the sharp ridge of the roof block.

10 A rigid craft knife can be used to cut the lead for the roof. Don't cut right through in one go. Instead, make a series of light scores along the line.

11 LEAD is surprisingly easy to work into shape. Use a block of wood to fold the edges over and mark with a knife again for the corners and edges. Avoid using a hammer, as this results in 'coining' (round dents).

Box-building variation

Mineralized felt, which is often used on shed roofs, would make an excellent alternative to lead for the roof.

12 IF you like, finish with an aerosol stain. Leave for at least 24 hours before putting the box out for the bugs.

Log bug house

This rustic bug house uses a handy piece of old log with holes drilled into it to attract invertebrates, and is topped off with lead to preserve it as well as a hook for hanging it up.

THERE couldn't be an easier project to make than this log bug house. There's something immensely satisfying about drilling lots of holes into a freshly cut log. Come to think of it, I quite enjoyed working the lead around the top as well. You can often find pieces of old log lying around woodland. This bug hotel is perfect for attracting ladybugs and lacewings – which feed on less welcome garden visitors such as aphids. To attract the most customers, hang the log in a sheltered spot and near to flowerbeds.

Species to expect

This log bug house might be colonized by:

UK species – wood-boring beetle larvae, spiders, ladybugs, lacewings, solitary bee species (including leafcutter, mason, sweat, wool-carding and carpenter bees).

US species – wood-boring beetle larvae, spiders, ladybugs, lacewings, solitary bee species (including leafcutter [right], mason, sweat, wool-carding and carpenter bees).

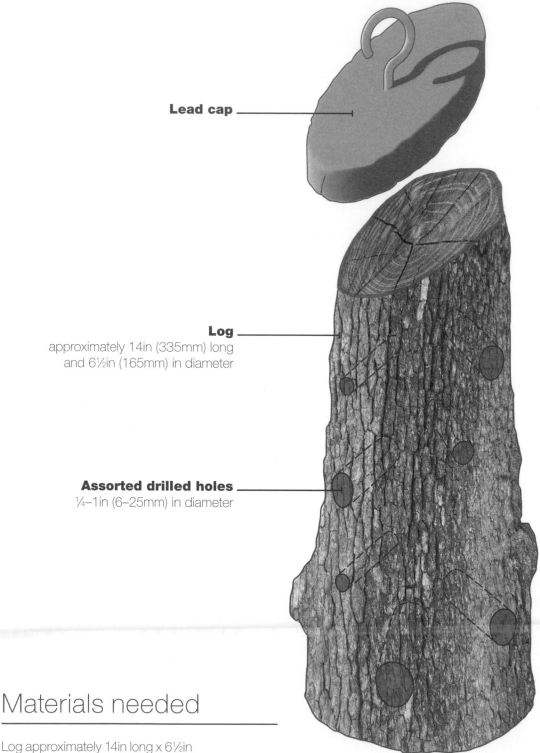

Lead cap

Log
approximately 14in (335mm) long
and 6½in (165mm) in diameter

Assorted drilled holes
¼–1in (6–25mm) in diameter

Materials needed

Log approximately 14in long x 6½in
diameter (355 x 165mm)
Lead sheeting offcut approximately
¹⁄₁₆in (1.5mm) thick
Large metal hook

1 SOURCE a suitable dry log with the bark on. Some of the insects that will seek refuge in it will want a hole 4–5in (100–127mm) deep. Therefore the log needs to be of sufficient thickness to allow you to bore to this depth.

2 IT will be easier to drill the holes if your log has a flat bottom, allowing it to stand upright on the workbench. Create a slope on the other end so that when the lead is placed on the top water will run off freely. Remove the sharp edge all around the top with some coarse sandpaper as this could damage the lead when it is being worked later.

3 START by drilling some large holes around the log; 1in (25mm) maximum will be big enough. You will need to leave space for at least three other hole sizes down to around ¼in (6mm) to allow for other species.

4 HOLD the log upright and make sure that the holes are drilled slightly uphill. This will prevent them from filling with water and drowning the occupants. Take care as well not to drill into other holes.

5 USING a craft knife, cut a square of lead larger than the top of the log and press it over the edges by hand to create an imprint of the shape in the lead.

6 USING a sturdy pair of domestic scissors, cut about ¾in (19mm) away from the imprint all the way around the lead.

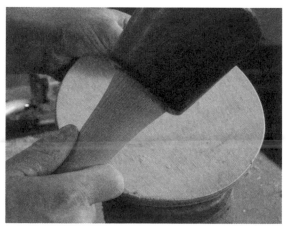

7 USE a block of wood and a mallet to beat the lead flat onto the sloping edge of the log. A round piece of plywood is a good choice; it allows you to see the edge as it is being worked and, unlike a small piece of solid timber, will not split after a few hefty wallops.

8 WITH a mallet, work the edge so that an even apron is created all the way round. Be careful not to over–work the lead as it can easily become too large and be a sloppy fit. Avoid hitting the edge as you may find you make a hole in the lead.

9 PROVIDING you have not worked the lead too much you should be left with just one crease.

10 MARK out and drill a hole in the centre of the top to take a large hook. To retain a water seal in the lead, inject a little silicone into the hole before screwing in the hook. Wipe away any excess silicone immediately with a cloth and some white spirit.

Box-building tip

A log house such as this one is quite heavy. If you decide to suspend it from a tree or outhouse, make sure it is well secured. Of course, it would be just as welcome located on the ground.

Four-slot bug house

This bug house is finished with a rough stone–effect paint to protect the ply, and provides a suitable home for ladybugs, lacewings and even butterflies and moths.

THIS bug house is simple to make and can be hung on a wall or fence. The slots provide routes of entry and exit for the insects and provide a place for ladybugs, lacewings, butterflies and moths to roost overnight or to lay their eggs. Encourage butterflies by placing twigs and an attractant, such as a small pot filled with a solution of water and sugar, in the interior. A Perspex flap allows you to view the box's occupants without disturbing them and to top up the butterfly attractant.

Species to expect

This bug house might become home to:

UK species – ladybugs, lacewings, butterflies and moths.

US species – ladybugs, lacewings, butterflies and moths.

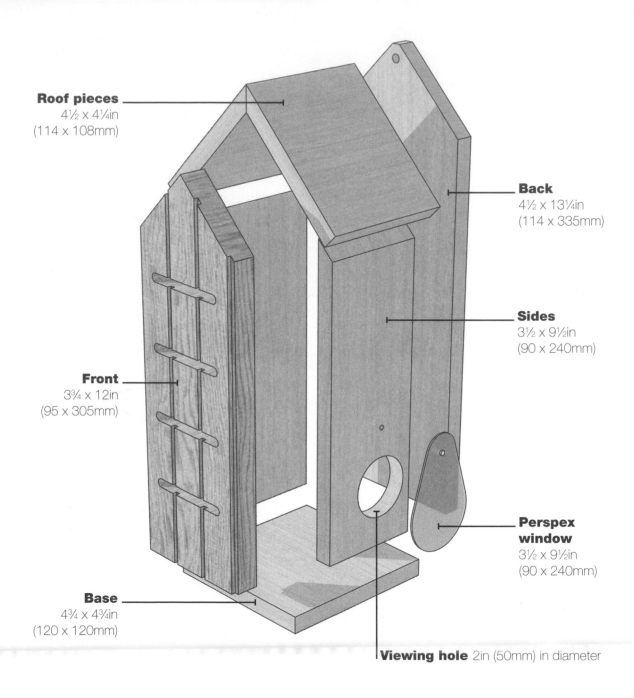

Roof pieces
4½ x 4¼in
(114 x 108mm)

Back
4½ x 13¼in
(114 x 335mm)

Sides
3½ x 9½in
(90 x 240mm)

Front
3¾ x 12in
(95 x 305mm)

Perspex window
3½ x 9½in
(90 x 240mm)

Base
4¾ x 4¾in
(120 x 120mm)

Viewing hole 2in (50mm) in diameter

Materials needed

½in (13mm) external plywood
¾in (19mm) softwood timber
Stone-effect external paint
Perspex

Cutting list

Back 4½ x 13¼in (114 x 335mm)
Sides 3½ x 9½in and trim (90 x 240mm)
Front 3¾ x 12in and trim (95 x 305mm)
Base 4¾ x 4¾in (120 x 120mm)
Roof 4½ x 4¼in (114 x 108mm)

1 ON the piece of softwood, use a mitre square to mark out the angle on the top for the roof at 45 degrees from the centre.

2 USE the front section to mark out the matching angles on the side components.

3 To check that the side components are exactly the same size, plane them together making sure not to let them slip when you turn them over.

4 GLUE and pin the sides to the front with an exterior-grade adhesive.

5 MARK out the slots and grooves on the front, avoiding the pins through the side.

6 WE used a router to create the slots, but you could just as easily drill a series of holes and make them into slots using a keyhole saw.

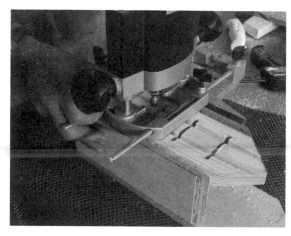

7 USE a router with a 'V' groove cutter to create the grooves in the front. This is purely for decoration.

8 GLUE and pin the base onto the box, keeping the back edge flush with the back of the box.

Box-building tip

Place one or two branch-like twigs inside this box to attract lacewings. To attract butterflies, finish the box in a brighter colour and place a sponge moistened with a sugar-and-water solution to tempt them inside.

9 TRIM the 45–degree angles on the top edge of the roof components, and glue and pin them in place to finish.

10 DRILL a hole in one side and cover with the Perspex disc. Finish as required (see page 29 for techniques). Allow the box to stand until the smell of the lacquer has gone before putting in its final location.

Box-building variation

As with most of the projects in this book, the materials used are not critical. This bug house, for example, could be made from timber sourced from old pallets or any other scavenged timber.

Multi-use bug house

A drilled split log forms the basis of this bug house, on top of which are amassed some bamboo canes of various sizes, enclosed in a wooden case to provide some shelter.

THIS bug house takes up quite a lot of material and requires a little extra skill to make. Although I used a router to create the slots, this could just as easily be done by drilling a series of holes close together and removing the waste with a chisel. You may also need to adapt the design to fit the dimensions of the split log and number of bamboo canes. This bug house should attract a range of interesting invertebrates, including solitary bees, lacewings, beetle larvae and ladybugs.

Species to expect

This bug house might offer shelter to:

UK species – wood-boring beetle larvae, spiders, ladybugs, lacewings (right), solitary bee species (including leafcutter, mason, sweat, wool-carding and carpenter bees).

US species – wood-boring beetle larvae, spiders, ladybugs, lacewings, solitary bee species (including leafcutter, mason, sweat, wool-carding and carpenter bees).

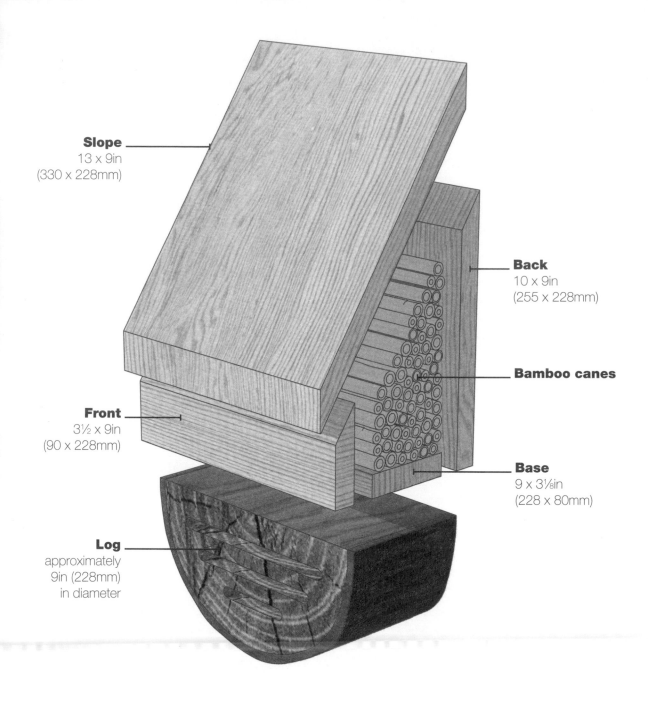

Slope
13 x 9in
(330 x 228mm)

Back
10 x 9in
(255 x 228mm)

Bamboo canes

Front
3½ x 9in
(90 x 228mm)

Base
9 x 3⅛in
(228 x 80mm)

Log
approximately
9in (228mm)
in diameter

Materials needed

Split log
Bamboo canes
Softwood timber

Cutting list

Back 10 x 9in (255 x 228mm) cut to size
Front 3½ x 9in (90 x 228mm) cut to size
Slope 13 x 9in (330 x 228mm) cut to size
Base 9 x 3⅛in (228 x 80mm)
Log 9in diameter (228mm)

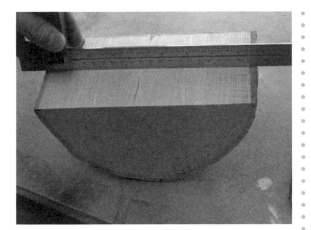

1 BEFORE you can prepare the cutting list for the top section, you need to prepare the base section, which is formed from a split log. The flat surface needs to be level in each direction.

2 OUR log was 9in (228mm) in diameter and 5in (127mm) thick, so our top section components were cut to suit. You may have to adjust your own dimensions.

4 WHEN you are happy that things line up, glue and clamp the pieces together; drive in a few nails for good measure.

3 CUT the 45-degree angles first; the square cut ends are easier to adjust to achieve accurate uprights.

5 TAKE the top slope piece and hold it in place with an overhang at the top. Using a straight edge or square, mark off the angle to cut so that it finishes in a clean point at the top.

6 GLUE and nail together as before, making sure the back components are all flush. This will ensure that the bug house sits tight up against the wall when it is hung in place.

7 MARK out the slots on the front face of the log parallel with the flat edge of the log.

Box-building tip

Be sure to make the joint between the two sections secure, since this bug house design can be quite heavy if made to the dimensions suggested above.

8 ON a log this size, three grooves were machined with a router using a ⅜in (9mm) bit to a depth of 1½in (38mm). Cutting the log accurately at the first stage makes using the router a quick option.

9 DRIVE screws in at an angle to fix the top sections to the log base.

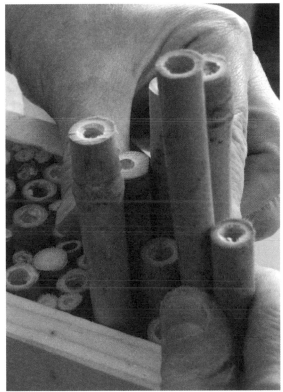

10 PACK in your twigs or bamboo pieces so that they are tight. With a good selection of canes or sticks you should not need to use any glue.

Box-building variation

Instead of routing grooves in the log, why not drill holes? You could also substitute bamboo canes for sunflower stems or dried cow-parsley stalks.

High-rise bug house

This bug house makes use of timber off-cuts otherwise destined for the log burner. 4 x 2in (100 x 50mm) is a common size of timber and is available in a variety of species.

THIS design of bug house uses the differing sizes of hole that attract different insect species to create an aesthetically pleasing ornament for your garden – but one with a wildlife-friendly purpose. The holes will attract solitary bees, beetles, ladybugs and lacewings among others, and the different hardnesses of wood will encourage more than one species. As with the other designs of bug houses, the wood should not be treated as this will harm the insects you are trying to attract. Hang the house in a sheltered spot by a wall or fence where it can catch the morning sun.

Species to expect

This bug house might attract:

UK species – wood-boring beetle larvae, spiders, ladybugs, lacewings, solitary bee species (including leafcutter, mason and carpenter bees).

US species – wood-boring beetle larvae, spiders, ladybugs (right), lacewings, solitary bee species (including leafcutter, mason and carpenter bees).

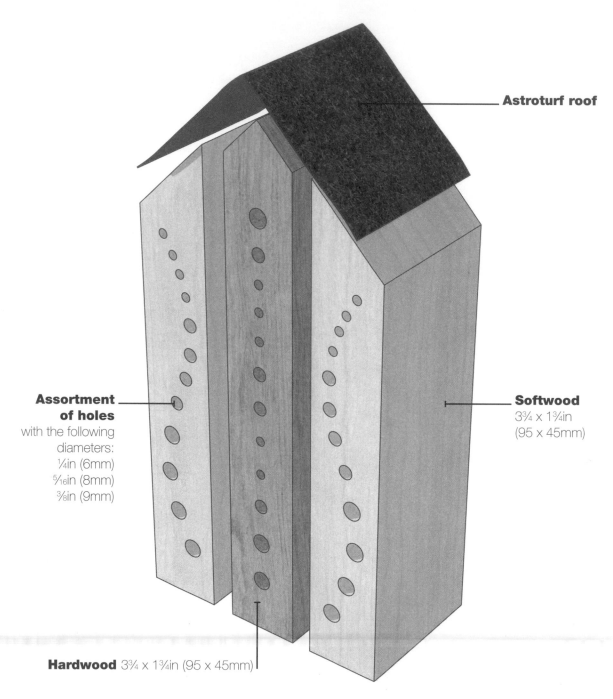

Astroturf roof

Assortment of holes
with the following diameters:
¼in (6mm)
⁵⁄₁₆in (8mm)
⅜in (9mm)

Softwood
3¾ x 1¾in
(95 x 45mm)

Hardwood 3¾ x 1¾in (95 x 45mm)

Materials needed

Softwood timber
Hardwood timber
Self-adhesive flooring tiles
Astroturf
Adhesive

Cutting list

2 x pieces of softwood timber
13½ x 3¾ x 1¾in (345 x 95 x 45mm)
1 x piece of hardwood timber
13½ x 3¾ x 1¾in (345 x 95 x 45mm)

Note: this size is often sold in timber merchants as 4 x 2in

1 FIRST check that the three pieces are of the same width before gluing them together with an exterior–grade adhesive. It helps to have all the pieces over–length so that the final block can be trimmed to length in one go later on.

2 IT may be necessary to smooth off after gluing up before marking out and cutting the angles for the roof.

3 FOR a fancy design, use a paper template to mark out the holes $^{13}/_{16}$in (22mm) apart.

4 TRANSFER the centres onto the block with a bradawl or other sharp tool. For simple lines, use a square and straight edge.

5 PREPARE to drill your holes at the same time. I used three different sizes to vary the pattern and to appeal to different sized bugs: ¼in (6mm), ⁵⁄₁₆in (8mm) and ⅜in (9mm).

6 IF you are doing this freehand, mark the depth of the hole by wrapping some tape around the drill bit.

7 THE tape acts as a depth stop to prevent you from bursting straight through to the other side of the block.

8 THE top of the block would benefit from being protected from the elements. One option would be to simply fix two further blocks of timber. As these are to be covered with some off-cuts of self-adhesive flooring tiles, make sure the nails are driven beneath the surface.

9 CUT the tiles over-size. Shape them after they have been fixed with either a small block plane or coarse abrasive paper.

10 OTHER materials, such as this piece of Astroturf, can be used and fixed down with a hot-glue gun.

Box-building variation

Instead of a pitched roof like this example, why not use a single slope with a clay roof tile on the top? If you intend to make use of any leftover timber from a building project, make sure that it has not been chemically treated.

shelved bug house

This is a more complicated bug house to build, with multiple, angled plywood shelves, but its value is in the richness and adaptability of home it can provide for your local insects.

THE open shelves of the bug house allow you to 'furnish' it using whatever materials come to hand. Filling the shelves with twigs, moss, cut grass or bark chippings will attract a variety of different invertebrates. Use clumps of straw to attract lacewings. The bark should attract ladybugs. Both insects and their larvae prey on troublesome aphids. Hang the bug house on a sheltered wall, fence or post in the sun and near flowerbeds with an aphid problem to provide your very own biological pesticide.

Species to expect

This bug house might offer accommodation to:

UK species – spiders, ladybugs, lacewings.

US species – spiders, ladybugs, lacewings.

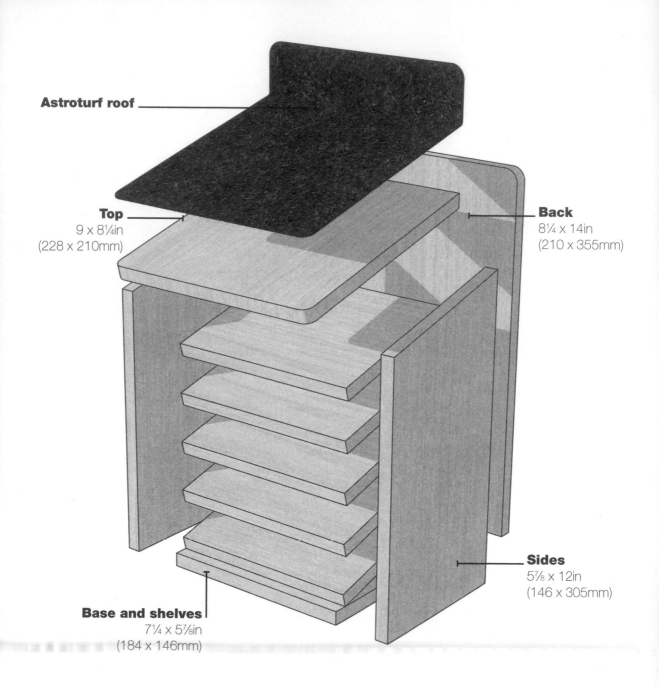

Astroturf roof

Top
9 x 8¼in
(228 x 210mm)

Back
8¼ x 14in
(210 x 355mm)

Sides
5⅞ x 12in
(146 x 305mm)

Base and shelves
7¼ x 5⅞in
(184 x 146mm)

Materials needed

½in (13mm) external plywood
Roofing felt or Astroturf

Cutting list

Back 8¼ x 14in (210 x 355mm)
Sides 5⅞ x 12in and trim (146 x 305mm)
Base 7¼ x 5⅞in (184 x 146mm)
Shelves 7¼ x 5⅞in (184 x 146mm)
Top 9 x 8¼in (228 x 210mm)

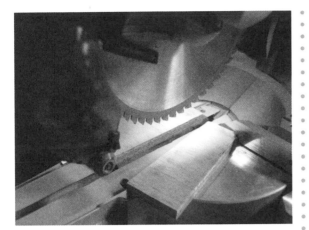

1 IF you can, use a machine to cut the plywood for this project. Nearly every face is visible, and a machine will give you cleaner edges. If you can't use a machine, score the lines first with a craft knife and cut as close to the line as possible. For a nice clean edge, you may need to use a plane as well.

2 HAVING cut all your components, set a sliding bevel to 15 degrees and begin to mark out the position of the shelves on one of the sides.

3 LAY the sides back to back and copy the lines over to the other side. Extend the lines to both faces of the side; this will help when it comes to nailing the box together.

4 GLUE the outer components together with exterior-grade adhesive and then pin them.

5 IT is unlikely you will be able to glue the shelves in place without making a slight mess along the way. Clean the glue off the shelves one at a time before fixing the next one.

6 NOW is a good time to run over the edges with a little sandpaper to remove all the unsightly pencil lines.

7 ROUND over the corners of the lid using a disc sander if you have one. This could also be done with a jigsaw fitted with a chipbreaker to minimize breakout.

8 BEFORE fixing the lid in place, create an angle on the back edge.

9 IF you intend to fix the box in place, you may wish to round off the corners of the back and drill some fixing holes as well.

10 LAY the box upside down on some roofing felt or Astroturf, and cut round using a craft knife.

Box-building tip

Although this bug house has a roof that is protected, the exposed edges of the ply will also need some protection. A water-based exterior finish is best. Anything else will need to dry completely until any nasty smells have gone. Choose a product that does not contain pesticides.

Resources

Useful organizations and websites

Birds
UK
www.bto.org (British Trust for Ornithology)
www.rspb.org.uk (Royal Society for the
Protection of Birds)

US
www.abcbirds.org (American Bird Conservancy)
www.audubon.org (National Audubon Society)

Bats
UK
www.bats.org.uk (Bat Conservation Trust)

US
www.batcon.org (Bat Conversation International)

Bees
UK
www.bumblebeeconservation.org.uk
(Bumblebee Conservation Trust)
www.helpsavebees.co.uk (Help Save Bees)
www.foxleas.com
www.insectpix.net

US
www.bumblebee.org

Bugs
UK
www.amentsoc.org
(Amateur Entomologists' Society)
www.buglife.org.uk
(The Invertebrate Conservation Trust)
www.butterfly–conservation.org
(Butterfly Conservation)

US
www.insectidentification.org
www.xerces.org (The Xerces Society for
Invertebrate Conservation)

General wildlife
UK
www.naturalengland.org.uk (Natural England)
www.wildlifetrusts.org (The Wildlife Trusts)

US
www.dcfcnders.org (Defenders of Wildlife)
www.wildlife.org (The Wildlife Society)

Useful books

Bat Boxes: A Guide to the History, Function, Construction and Use in the Conservation of Bats RE Stebbings and ST Walsh: Bat Conservation Society, 1997

Bird Boxes and Feeders: Stylish Designs for Attracting Birds Alan Bridgewater, Gill Bridgewater and Stephen Moss: New Holland, 2001

Bird Boxes and Feeders for the Garden Dave Mackenzie: Guild of Master Craftsman Publications, 1997

Birdhouses John Kelsey: PRC Publishing, 2002

Chris Packham's Back Garden Nature Reserve Chris Packham: New Holland, 2010

How to Create a Wildlife Garden Christine Lavelle and Michael Lavelle: Frances Lincoln, 2000

How to Make a Wildlife Garden Chris Baines: Frances Lincoln, 2000

RSPB Gardening for Wildlife: A Complete Guide to Nature-friendly Gardening Adrian Thomas: A & C Black, 2010

The Butterfly-Friendly Garden John and Maureen Tampion: Guild of Master Craftsman Publications, 2010

The Birdwatcher's Garden Hazel Johnson and Pamela Johnson: Guild of Master Craftsman Publications, 2010

The BTO Nestbox Guide Chris du Feu: British Trust for Ornithology, 2003

Wildlife Habitats for Your Garden Josie Briggs: Guild of Master Craftsman Publications, 2010

Suppliers

The projects in this book use tools and materials that can all be easily sourced from your local hardware store or timber yard. No specialist suppliers will be required and indeed many of the materials you use may be salvaged, recycled or left over from other projects. Below is a list of larger chain stores that can be found in the UK and US.

UK

B&Q
www.diy.com

Travis Perkins
www.travisperkins.co.uk

Homebase
www.homebase.co.uk

Wickes
www.wickes.co.uk

Jewson
www.jewson.co.uk

Build Center
www.buildcenter.co.uk

US

Lowe's
www.lowes.com

Ace Hardware
www.acehardware.com

Home Depot
www.homedepot.com

USA Hardware
www.usahardware.com

Index

To place an order, or to request a catalogue, contact:
GMC Publications, Castle Place, 166 High Street, Lewes,
East Sussex, BN7 1XU United Kingdom
Tel: +44 (0)1273 488005 Fax: +44 (0)1273 402866
Website: www.gmcbooks.com
Orders by credit card are accepted